PEGASUS SHAKESPEARE BIBLIOGRAPHIES

RICHARD L. NOCHIMSON
Yeshiva University
General Editor

Shakespeare and the Renaissance Stage
to 1616
Shakespearean Stage History
1616 to 1998

An Annotated Bibliography
of Shakespeare Studies
1576–1998

PEGASUS SHAKESPEARE BIBLIOGRAPHIES

RICHARD L. NOCHIMSON
Yeshiva University
General Editor

Shakespeare and the Renaissance Stage
to 1616
Shakespearean Stage History
1616 to 1998

An Annotated Bibliography
of Shakespeare Studies
1576–1998

HUGH MACRAE RICHMOND
Editor

Pegasus Press
University of North Carolina at Asheville
Asheville, NC
1999

© Copyright 1999
Pegasus Press
Asheville, North Carolina

Library of Congress Cataloguing-in-Publication Data

Shakespeare and the Renaissance stage to 1616 and Shakespearean stage history 1616 to 1998 : an annotated bibliography of Shakespeare studies, 1576–1998 / Hugh M. Richmond, editor.
    p. cm. — (Pegasus Shakespeare bibliographies)
  Includes indexes.
  ISBN 1-889818-22-4 (alk. paper)
  1. Shakespeare, William, 1564–1616—Stage history—To 1625—Bibliography. 2. Shakespeare, William, 1564–1616—Dramatic production—Bibliography. 3. Shakespeare, William, 1564–1616—Stage history—Bibliography. 4. Theater—England—History—Bibliography. 5. Renaissance—England—Bibliography. I. Richmond, Hugh M. II. Series.

Z8813 .S47 1999
[PR3095]
016.7929'5—dc21

                                                                               99-049464

This book is made to last.
It is printed on acid-free paper
to library specifications.

Contents

Preface ... vii

    List of Abbreviations ... xi

I. Editions of Shakespeare's Plays and Basic Reference Works

    A. Single-Volume Editions of Shakespeare's Plays ... 1
    B. Multi-Volume Editions of Shakespeare's Plays ... 5
    C. Basic Reference Works for Shakespeare Studies ... 9

II. Shakespeare & the Renaissance Stage to 1616

    A. General Studies of the Elizabethan Theatre ... 19
    B. The Physical Characteristics of Elizabethan Theatres ... 36
        1. Background Studies ... 36
        2. Shakespeare's Theatres ... 40
    C. Shakespeare & Elizabethan Theatrical Practices ... 46

III. Shakespearean Stage History: 1616–1998

    A. Overviews: 1616–1998 ... 64
    B. Early Performances: 1616–1642 ... 76
    C. The Interregnum: 1660–1837 ... 78
        1. General Studies ... 78
        2. Individual Managers and Actors ... 85
    D. Modern Performances: 1837–1998 ... 90
        1. General Studies ... 90
        2. The Victorians and Edwardians: 1837–1914 ... 96
        3. World War I to World War II: 1914–1945 ... 101
        4. The Contemporary Period: 1945–1998 ... 106
        5. Shakespeare on Film and Video ... 124
    E. Pedagogy ... 133

Index I: Authors and Editors ... 138

Index II: Subjects ... 145

Abbreviations

All's Well	*All's Well That Ends Well*
Antony	*Antony and Cleopatra*
c.	about
Caesar	*Julius Caesar*
chap., chaps.	chapter(s)
comp.	complier / compiled by
Dream	*A Midsummer Night's Dream*
ed., eds.	edited by / editor(s)
e.g.	for example
Errors	*The Comedy of Errors*
et al.	and others
i.e.	that is
John	*King John*
Kinsmen	*The Two Noble Kinsmen*
Lear	*King Lear*
Love's Labour's	*Love's Labour's Lost*
Merchant	*The Merchant of Venice*
Merry Wives	*The Merry Wives of Windsor*
Much Ado	*Much Ado About Nothing*
no., nos.	number(s)
n.s.	new series
p., pp.	page(s)
repr.	reprint / reprinted
rev.	revised
Romeo	*Romeo and Juliet*
Shrew	*The Taming of the Shrew*
SQ	*Shakespeare Quarterly*
Timon	*Timon of Athens*
Titus	*Titus Andronicus*
trans.	translated by
Troilus	*Troilus and Cressida*
Two Gentlemen	*The Two Gentlemen of Verona*
Univ.	University
vol., vols.	volume(s)

Preface

The twelve volumes of this series, of which this is the fifth, are designed to provide a guide to secondary materials important for the study of Shakespeare—not only for scholars but also for graduate and undergraduate students and for college and high school teachers. In nine of the twelve volumes, entries will refer to materials that focus on individual works by Shakespeare; a total of twenty-five plays, plus *The Rape of Lucrece*, will be covered in these volumes. The current volume is one of three that will present materials that treat Shakespeare in more general ways. This is a highly selective bibliography. While making sure to represent different approaches to the study of Shakespeare, the editors are including only work that is either of high quality or of great influence.

In this particular volume, there was special need to be extremely selective, and many worthy texts are not included. Because of the coverage of performances of specific Shakespeare plays in other volumes in this series, no texts dealing with production of a single play are recorded here. Also, many worthy broader texts have been omitted because the principle of inclusion has been to seek recent, current, comprehensive, authoritative, and influential texts, with a preference for those from which further research in specific areas can be most readily extended (e.g., fully annotated and indexed texts with significant bibliographies of their own). Only the most significant editions of reprinted texts are cited. A few distinctive sources from earlier periods (Henslowe, Heywood, etc.) are included because of their continuing relevance to research. For a variety of reasons, this volume is limited to works available in English. Recognition of sustained achievement in Shakespeare production from outside the English-speaking world occurs only where such productions are accessible within it and have received substantial discussion, as with the film work of Kozintsev and Kurosawa.

In this volume, entries for the works included are numbered consecutively throughout the volume. Within each subsection, entries are organized alphabetically by author.

Each entry contains the basic factual information and a brief annotation. Since inclusion of a book or article in this bibliography implies a positive evaluation, the annotations are designed to be descriptive primarily rather than evaluative. The intention is to convey to the reader the contents of the work being annotated. Readers will find that where evaluative comments could not be resisted they appear at the end of an annotation.

The organization of this volume is as follows:

Section I, which will be essentially the same in all twelve volumes, contains those editions and general reference works that in the collective opinion of the editors are most basic to the study of Shakespeare. The annotations in this section have been written by the following series editors: Jean E. Howard, Clifford C. Huffman, John S. Mebane (who has undertaken the updating as well as the composing of the annotations in subsections A and B), Richard L. Nochimson, Hugh M. Richmond, Barbara H. Traister, and John W. Velz.

Section II is devoted to material concerning the Renaissance stage up to the time of Shakespeare's death in 1616. Section III deals with Shakespearean stage history from 1616 to the present. Each of these sections is divided into several subsection; the kinds of works represented by these subsections are described in the table of contents. In Section III, the subsection for the chronological period 1660–1837 is identified as "the Interregnum," because of its characteristic indifference in performance to the authority of Shakespeare's texts as originally published.

Some items, of course, cannot be neatly categorized under the heading of a single subsection. When an item could easily fall into more than one subsection, the editor of this volume has placed the item in the most appropriate subsection, and has cross-referenced it at the end of the other relevant subsections. For example, a relevant book for Elizabethan and Jacobean staging listed in Section I, such as no. 20, Andrew Gurr's *The Shakespearean Stage 1574–1642*, is cited at the end of Section II's Subsections A, B1, B2, C, and of Section III's Subsection B. Readers should consult the cross-references at the end of each subsection as well as the subject index (where items are listed by item number only), to see the full range of material relevant to a particular area or topic.

In general, items in this bibliography are not given more than one bibliographical entry. Exceptions to this rule occur when a comprehensive study includes an item of distinct significance needing fuller treatment than the study's numerous other elements permit. For example, no. 154, G.E. Bentley's *The Seventeenth Century Stage: A Collection of Critical Essays*, includes no. 114, W. Ringler, "The Number of Actors in Shakespeare's Early Plays," an essay which is crucial to all discussion of casting in Shakespeare's time. Many of the texts noted here have appeared in numerous editions; in general, this volume cites the first date and location at which a text appeared in its current form. This reference may be either to the first edition that stands unmodified as the accepted final form (probably the latest revision by the author) or to the most substantial edition thereafter if its scholarly apparatus enhances its value.

Within the entries, numbers prefaced by "no." indicate cross-references; numbers in parentheses indicate either the page numbers in the book or article where a specific topic is discussed or quoted, or the act, scene, and line numbers of the passage discussed, divided by periods, (e.g., 5.5.45–50). For convenience, unless specified otherwise, the act, scene, and line designations are taken from *The Riverside Shakespeare* (no. 2).

Abbreviations are listed on the next page.

The editors would like to thank all their colleagues, friends, and family members who helped in innumerable ways with the preparation of this bibliography.

Hugh M. Richmond
University of California, Berkeley

Richard L. Nochimson
Yeshiva University

October 1998

I. Editions and Reference Works

A. Single-Volume Editions

1. **Bevington, David, ed.** *The Complete Works of Shakespeare.* Updated 4th edition. New York: Addison Wesley Longman, 1997.

Bevington's *Complete Works* includes 38 plays and the nondramatic poems. Introductions, aimed at a broad audience, focus upon questions of interpretation. The general introduction discusses social, intellectual, and theatrical history; Shakespeare's biography and his career as a dramatist; his language and versification; editions and editors of Shakespeare; and the history of Shakespearean criticism. Appendices include discussions of canon, dates, and early texts; brief summaries of sources; and performance history. There are genealogical charts, maps, and a selected bibliography. Emendations of the copy text are recorded only in an appendix; they are not bracketed in the texts of the plays. Spelling is modernized unless an exception is necessary for scansion, to indicate a pun, or for other reasons discussed in the preface. Notes appear at the bottom of the column. Speech prefixes are expanded. Illustrations include photographs from recent performances. Features ranging from the clarity and high quality of the introductions to the readability of the typeface combine to make the texts in this edition admirably accessible to students and general readers. Available with this edition are the BBC's CD-ROM programs on *Macbeth* and *A Midsummer Night's Dream*. These multimedia resources provide the full text and complete audio recordings; footnotes; word and image searches; sources; comments and audio-visual aids on plot, themes, language, performance history, historical background, and characterization; print capability; and clips from film and video performances. A *Teacher's*

Guide to the CD provides suggestions for assignments and classroom use.

2. **Evans, G. Blakemore, et al., eds.** *The Riverside Shakespeare.* 2nd edition. Boston: Houghton Mifflin, 1997.

This edition includes 39 plays, the nondramatic poems, and segments of *Sir Thomas More*. Introductions by Herschel Baker (histories), Frank Kermode (tragedies), Hallett Smith (romances and nondramatic poems), Anne Barton (comedies), and J. J. M. Tobin ("A Funeral Elegy" by W. S. and *Edward III*) discuss dates, sources, and major interpretive issues. Harry Levin's general introduction discusses Shakespeare's biography, artistic development, and reputation; intellectual backgrounds; Renaissance playhouses and theatrical conventions; Elizabethan English; and stylistic techniques. Heather Dubrow provides an analytical survey of twentieth-century Shakespeare criticism. Evans provides an introduction to textual criticism. Appendices include a history of Shakespearean performance by Charles H. Shattuck and William T. Liston; substantial excerpts from historical documents related to Shakespeare's life and works, including some early responses to the plays; "Annals, 1552–1616," a listing in four parallel columns of events in political history, Shakespeare's biography, theater history, and nondramatic literature; a selected bibliography; indexes; and a glossary. Emendations of the copy text are enclosed in square brackets, and each play is followed by a summary discussion of editorial problems and by textual notes listing the sources of all emendations. Spelling is modernized except for "a selection of Elizabethan spelling forms that reflect . . . contemporary pronunciation" (67). Notes appear at the bottom of the column. The volume includes numerous illustrations, including color plates. While the *Riverside* has many features aimed at general readers, the impressive textual apparatus, Evans's fine discussion of textual criticism, and the collection of documents make this edition of special interest to advanced graduate students and to scholars.

3. **Greenblatt, Stephen, Walter Cohen, Jean E. Howard, and Katharine Eisaman Maus, eds.** *The Norton Shakespeare, Based on the Oxford Edition.* New York: Norton, 1997.

This edition includes 38 plays (including quarto, folio, and conflated texts of *King Lear*) and the nondramatic poems, including works of uncertain authorship not included in other single-volume editions. The texts (except for "A Funeral Elegy," ed. Donald Foster) are updated versions of those in the modern-spelling, single-volume *Oxford Shakespeare* (1988) produced by general editors Stanley Wells and Gary Taylor with John Jowett and William Montgomery. The *Oxford* edition is based on revisionary editorial principles, including the belief that some texts previously regarded as having limited authority are in reality records (at times highly imperfect) of early authorial versions later revised in the theater. The revised versions are usually chosen as control texts. In the *Oxford*, passages from earlier versions are often reprinted in appendices; the *Norton* prints these passages from earlier versions, indented, within the texts. *The Norton Shakespeare* provides marginal glosses and numerous explanatory notes; the latter are numbered in the text and appear at the bottom of each page. Textual variants are listed after each work. Stage directions added after the 1623 Folio appear in brackets. Greenblatt's general introduction discusses Renaissance economic, social, religious, and political life; Shakespeare's biography; textual criticism; and aspects of Shakespeare's art, including "The Paradoxes of Identity" in characterization and analysis of the "overpowering exuberance and generosity" (63) of Shakespeare's language. Introductions to individual works discuss a range of historical and aesthetic issues. Appendices include Andrew Gurr's "The Shakespearean Stage"; a collection of documents; a chronicle of events in political and literary history; a bibliography; and a glossary. This edition combines traditional scholarship with a focus on such recent concerns as the status of women and "The English and Otherness." Also available is *The Norton Shakespeare Workshop*, ed. Mark Rose, a set of interactive multimedia programs on CD-ROM that can be purchased either separately or in a package with *The Norton Shakespeare*. The *Workshop* provides searchable texts of *A Midsummer Night's Dream; The Merchant of Venice; Henry IV, Part Two; Othello; Hamlet; The Tempest;* and sonnets 55 and 138. Students can find analyses of selected passages, sources, essays that illustrate the play's critical and performance history; clips from classic and from specially commissioned performances, selections of music inspired by the plays, and tools for developing paper topics.

4. **Hinman, Charlton, ed.** *The Norton Facsimile: The First Folio of Shakespeare.* 2nd edition. Introduction by Peter Blayney. New York: W. W. Norton, 1996.

The First Folio of 1623 is a collection of 36 plays made by Shakespeare's fellow actors, Heminge and Condell. *Pericles, The Two Noble Kinsmen*, and the nondramatic poems are not included. Heminge and Condell claim to have provided "perfect" texts, distinguishing them from what they describe as "stolne, and surreptitious copies, maimed, and deformed by the frauds and stealthes of injurious impostors" (A3). While some of the previously published quartos are regarded today as superior versions, the First Folio indeed provides the most authoritative texts for the majority of Shakespeare's plays. It also includes commendatory poems by four authors, including Ben Jonson, and the Droeshout portrait of Shakespeare. During the two years that the 1623 edition was in press, corrections were made continually, and the uncorrected pages became mingled with corrected ones. In addition, imperfections of various sorts render portions of numerous pages difficult or impossible to read. Hinman has examined the 80 copies of the First Folio in the Folger Shakespeare Library and selected the clearest versions of what appear to be the finally corrected pages. In the left and right margins, he provides for reference his system of "through line numbering," by which he numbers each typographical line throughout the text of a play (the verse and prose of the play as well as all other material such as scene headings and stage directions). In a page from *King John*, for example, which includes what might otherwise be referred to as 3.1.324 through 3.3.74 (this form of reference appears in the bottom margin), the through line numbers run from 1257 to 1380. Appendix A presents some variant states of the Folio text, and Appendix B lists the Folger copies used in compiling this edition. Hinman's introduction discusses the nature and authority of the Folio, the printing and proofreading process, and the procedures followed in editing the facsimile, explaining, among other points, the advantages of through line numbering. Blayney's introduction updates Hinman's discussions of such matters as the status of quarto texts, the types of play-manuscripts available to printers, and the printing and proofreading processes. Blayney also discusses the theory that, since different versions of a given play may represent authorial or collaborative revisions, in such cases there is no "ideal text." No interpretive introductions or glosses are provided. While some valuable facsimiles of quarto versions are available, the Hinman First Folio is clearly an excellent place to begin one's encounter with early printed texts that are not mediated by centuries of editorial tradition.

B. Multi-Volume Editions

5. **Barnet, Sylvan, general ed.** *The Signet Classic Shakespeare.* New York: Penguin.

Originally edited in the 1960s, the Signet series was updated in the 1980s; newly revised volumes began to appear in 1998. The 35-volume series includes 38 plays and the nondramatic poems. Collections entitled *Four Great Comedies, Four Great Tragedies,* and *The Sonnets and Nondramatic Poems* are available. Each volume includes a general introduction with discussions of Shakespeare's biography, including the "anti-Stratfordian" authorship phenomenon; Shakespeare's English; Elizabethan theaters; "Shakespeare's Dramatic Language: Costumes, Gestures and Silences; Prose and Poetry"; editorial principles; and the staging of Shakespeare's plays, including consideration of the concept of the play as a collaboration among the playwright, theatrical ensemble, and audience. Spelling is generally modernized, and speech prefixes are expanded. Explanatory notes appear at the bottom of each page. Appendices contain textual notes, discussion of (and often excerpts from) sources, several critical essays, a survey of each play's performance history, and a bibliography. Although introductions in this series are written for beginning students, the substantial selection of distinguished critical essays is useful for more advanced students, as well.

6. **Bevington, David, ed.** David Scott Kastan, James Hammersmith, and Robert Kean Turner, associate eds. *The Bantam Shakespeare.* New York: Bantam, 1988.

In 1988, 37 plays and the nondramatic poems were published in the 29 volumes of *The Bantam Shakespeare*. Collections entitled *Four Comedies* and *Four Tragedies* are available. Texts, explanatory notes (at the bottom of each page), and interpretive introductions are similar to those of Bevington's *Complete Works of Shakespeare* (see no. 1). Included in the Bantam series are brief performance histories of individual plays and Joseph Papp's forewords on Shakespeare's enduring appeal. Each volume includes a one-page biography of Shakespeare and an introduction to Elizabethan playhouses. Appendices include concise discussions of dates and early texts, textual notes, substantial excerpts from sources, and a brief annotated bibliography. While this series necessarily excludes some of the historical information found in the *Complete Works*, the forewords by an eminent producer/director and the well-written performance histories are engaging features, especially appropriate for students and general readers.

7. **Brockbank, Philip, founding general ed.** Brian Gibbons, general ed. A. R. Braunmuller and R. C. Hood, associate general eds. *The New Cambridge Shakespeare*. Cambridge: Cambridge Univ. Press, 1982–.

The New Cambridge series will eventually include 39 plays (with *The Reign of Edward III*) and the nondramatic poems. So far, 33 volumes have appeared; among these are two separate editions (one based on an early quarto) of *King Lear*, of *Hamlet*, and of *Richard III*. Introductions discuss date, sources, critical history and interpretive issues, staging, and performance history (with numerous illustrations). Discussion of the text precedes each play, and more detailed textual analysis sometimes appears in an appendix. All volumes include a selected bibliography. Spelling is generally modernized; speech prefixes are expanded. Textual notes signaling departures from the copy text and extensive explanatory notes appear at the bottom of each page. Designed for students and scholars, *The New Cambridge Shakespeare* provides more detailed attention to stagecraft and performance history than most other editions. This series succeeds *The New Shakespeare*, edited by Arthur Quiller-Couch and John Dover Wilson.

EDITIONS AND REFERENCE WORKS   7

8. **Knowles, Richard, and Paul Werstine, general eds.** Robert K. Turner, senior consulting editor. *A New Variorum Edition of Shakespeare.* New York: Modern Language Association.

From 1871 to 1928 H. H. Furness, Sr., and H. H. Furness, Jr., published 19 works of the Variorum Shakespeare. Since 1933, nine new editions have appeared in the MLA series. The completed 40-volume variorum will contain 38 plays and the nondramatic poems. Each volume provides an old-spelling text and a collation of significant emendations from previous editions. Explanatory notes (printed below the textual notes at the bottom of each page) try to record all important previous annotation. Appendices include discussions of a play's text and date. Recent volumes survey the history of criticism and performance and refer to a substantial bibliography; early volumes include excerpts from previous criticism. Sources and analogues are discussed and reprinted. As compilations of scholarship, criticism, and textual analysis, these volumes represent a significant resource for scholars and teachers.

9. **Mowat, Barbara A., and Paul Werstine, eds.** *The New Folger Library Shakespeare.* New York: Pocket Books, Washington Square Press, 1992–.

Nineteen volumes of the New Folger series, which replaces *The Folger Library General Reader's Shakespeare*, appeared between 1992 and 1997. Several new titles will come out each year until the series of 38 plays and the nondramatic poems is complete. Each volume provides a brief initial comment on the play followed by basic introductions to Shakespeare's language and style, his biography, Elizabethan theaters, early editions, and the editorial principles of the series. Half brackets enclose emendations of the copy text; in some volumes square or pointed brackets indicate the sources of passages that appear (for example) only in the folio or an earlier quarto. Explanatory notes appear on pages facing the text, textual notes in an appendix. Spelling is selectively modernized, and speech prefixes are expanded. For each play a different critic offers the "Modern Perspective" that follows the text. A brief annotated bibliography focuses mostly on recent approaches to the play; standard works on language, biography, theatrical setting, and early texts also appear. While this series aims at the broadest possible audience, the clarity and helpfulness of its introductions and explanatory notes make it especially well suited for beginning students.

10. **Proudfoot, Richard, Ann Thompson, and David Scott Kastan, general eds.** *The Arden Shakespeare.* Walton-on-Thames, Surrey: Nelson House.

The 40-volume *Arden Shakespeare* includes 38 plays and 2 volumes of the nondramatic poems. The edition is continually updated; although some current volumes are from the 1950s, nine plays and the Sonnets have appeared in revised third editions in recent years. Introductions provide extensive discussion of dates, texts, editorial principles, sources, and a wide range of interpretive issues. Extensive textual and explanatory notes appear at the bottom of each page. Appendices typically include additional textual analysis, excerpts from sources, and (sometimes) settings for songs. The Arden series often includes scholarship and criticism that is essential for advanced students and scholars. The complete second edition of the Arden series is available on CD-ROM from Primary Source Media. The CD-ROMs enable one to view the edited texts simultaneously with materials from the following: early quarto and folio editions; Bullough's *Narrative and Dramatic Sources* (no. 15); Abbott's *Shakespearian Grammar*; Onions's *Shakespeare Glossary* (no. 21); Partridge's *Shakespeare's Bawdy*; and a 4,600-item bibliography.

11. **Spencer, T. J. B., general ed.** Stanley Wells, associate ed. *The New Penguin Shakespeare.* London: Penguin Books.

The 39-volume New Penguin series now includes 36 plays and the nondramatic poems; *Titus Andronicus* and *Cymbeline* are planned. Dates range from the 1960s through the 1980s. Introductions discuss a range of interpretive issues and are followed by brief bibliographical essays. Explanatory notes follow the text, succeeded by textual analysis, selective textual notes, and (as appropriate) settings for songs. Spelling is modernized, and speech prefixes are expanded. Emendations of the copy text are not bracketed. The New Penguin will appeal especially to those who wish the pages of the text to be free of annotation.

12. **Wells, Stanley, general ed.** Advisory eds. S. Schoenbaum, G. R. Proudfoot, and F. W. Sternfeld. *The Oxford Shakespeare.* Oxford: Oxford Univ. Press.

Between 1982 and 1996, 23 plays (plus collections entitled *Comedies, Histories,* and *Tragedies*) were published in the multivolume *Oxford Shakespeare.* The completed series will include 38 plays and the nondramatic poems. Introductions provide detailed discussion of dates, sources, textual criticism, questions of interpretation, and performance history. Textual notes and extensive commentary appear at the bottom of each page. The commentary and introduction are indexed. Spelling is modernized, and speech prefixes are expanded. The Oxford series is based on revisionary editorial principles, including the belief that some texts previously regarded as of little value are in reality records (at times highly imperfect) of early authorial versions later revised in the theater. The revised versions are usually chosen as copy texts, and appendices sometimes include passages from earlier printed versions. Some appendices include musical settings for songs. Partly because of its editorial principles, this series is of special interest to scholars and advanced students.

C. Basic Reference Works for Shakespeare Studies

13. **Beckerman, Bernard.** *Shakespeare at the Globe: 1599–1609.* New York: Macmillan, 1962.

This study of the 29 extant plays (including 15 by Shakespeare) produced at the Globe in its first decade yields information about the playhouse and how Shakespeare's company performed in it. The first chapter, on the repertory system, is based on analysis of Henslowe's diary. Subsequent chapters about the stage itself, acting styles, the dramatic form of plays and of scenes within plays, and the staging derive from study of the Globe repertory. Detailed appendices provide statistics on which Beckerman's analysis partly depends. Beckerman concludes that the style in which these plays were presented was neither symbolic nor what modern audiences would call realistic. Rather, he suggests, passion by the actors was presented within a framework of staging and scenic conventions in various styles according to the needs of particular plays.

14. **Bentley, G. E.** *The Jacobean and Caroline Stage.* 7 vols. Oxford: Clarendon Press, 1941–68.

Bentley designed his survey of British drama to carry on that of Chambers (see no. 16) and cover the years 1616–42. The 11 chapters in vol. 1 provide detailed information about 11 adult and children's acting companies (1–342); vol. 2 surveys information about actors, listed alphabetically (343–629), with relevant documents reprinted and annotated (630–96), with an index (697–748). Vols. 3, 4, 5 are an alphabetical list, by author, with bibliographical material and commentary, of "all plays, masques, shows, and dramatic entertainments which were written or first performed in England between 1616 . . . and . . . 1642" (3.v), from "M.A." to Richard Zouche, with a final section (5. 1281–1456) on anonymous and untitled plays. Vol. 6 considers theater buildings (private, 3–117; public, 121–252; court, 255–88; and two that were only projected, 291–309). Vol. 7 gathers together, as appendices to vol. 6, "scattered material concerning Lenten performances and Sunday performances" and arranges chronologically "a large number of dramatic and semi-dramatic events" of interest to students of dramatic literature and theater history (6.v); it includes a general index for vols. 1–7 (129–390) which has numerous references (344–45) to Shakespeare and his plays.

15. **Bullough, Geoffrey.** *Narrative and Dramatic Sources of Shakespeare.* 8 vols. London and New York: Routledge & Kegan Paul and Columbia Univ. Press, 1957–75.

This work is a comprehensive compendium of the texts of Shakespeare's sources for 37 plays and several poems. Bullough includes analogues as well as sources and "possible sources" as well as "probable sources." All texts are in English, old-spelling Elizabethan when extant, and in some other cases in the compiler's translation. Bullough includes a separate introduction for each play. In the early volumes, interpretation is largely left to the reader; introductions in the later volumes include more interpretation and tend to be longer. There have been complaints of occasional errors in transcription. The major caveat, however, about using this learned, thorough, and imaginative work concerns what Bullough could not conceivably print: the passages in his sources that Shakespeare presumably read but either chose to omit or neglected to include.

16. **Chambers, E. K.** *The Elizabethan Stage.* 4 vols. Oxford: Clarendon Press, 1923. Revised 1945; with corrections 1967.

In vol. 1, Chambers provides detailed information about the court (1–234): the monarchs, their households, the Revels Office, pageantry, the mask, and the court play. In the section entitled "The Control of the Stage" (236–388), he covers the struggles between the city of London and the court and between Humanism and Puritanism, and treats the status of actors and the socioeconomic realities of actors' lives. In vol. 2, Chambers focuses on the history of 38 different acting companies (children, adult, and foreign) (1–294), gives details, such as are known, about an alphabetical list of actors (295–350), and treats the playhouses (16 public and 2 private theaters), including discussion of their structure and management (351–557). In vol. 3, Chambers surveys the conditions of staging in the court and theaters (1–154), the printing of plays (157–200), and then offers a bibliographical survey, including brief biographies, of playwrights alphabetically arranged, from William Alabaster through Christopher Yelverton (201–518). In vol. 4, Chambers concludes that bibliography with anonymous work (1–74) and presents 13 appendices that reprint or summarize relevant historical documents. Chambers concludes this work with four indexes (to plays, persons, places, and subjects) to the four volumes (409–67). In these four volumes, Chambers presents an encyclopedia of all aspects of English drama during the reigns of Elizabeth I and James I up to the date of Shakespeare's death in 1616. A subsequent and detailed index to this entire work was compiled by Beatrice White, *An Index to "The Elizabethan Stage" and "William Shakespeare" by Sir Edmund Chambers.* Oxford: Oxford Univ. Press, 1934.

17. **Chambers, E. K.** *William Shakespeare: A Study of Facts and Problems.* 2 vols. Oxford: Clarendon Press, 1930. Repr., 1931.

This work is an encyclopedia of information relating to

Shakespeare. The principal topics of the first volume are the dramatist's family origins, his relations to the theater and its professionals, the nature of the texts of his plays—including their preparation for performance and publication, and also questions of authenticity and chronology (relevant tables about the quartos and metrics are in the second volume). The data available (and plausible conjectures) concerning all texts attributed to Shakespeare, including poems and uncertain attributions, are then laid out title by title. The second volume cites the significant Shakespeare records then available, including contemporary allusions, performance data, legends, and even forgeries (the last two items are more fully covered in Schoenbaum's *Shakespeare's Lives*). There are comprehensive indices and a substantial bibliography. While it is sometimes necessary to update this book by correlation with Schoenbaum's *Documentary Life* (see no. 23) and other, more recent, texts, Chambers's scholarship has been supplemented rather than invalidated by more recent research, and his work remains a convenient starting point for pursuit of background data on Shakespeare's life and works.

18. **Doran, Madeleine.** *Endeavors of Art: A Study of Form in Elizabethan Drama.* Madison: Univ. of Wisconsin Press, 1954.

Doran reconstructs the Elizabethan assumptions about many aspects of dramatic form, defined broadly enough to include genre, eloquence and copiousness, character, and "moral aim." A detailed exploration of classical, medieval, and Renaissance backgrounds makes this a study in historical criticism; however, the cultural context laid out is aesthetic, not ideational. Doran examines the problems of form faced by Shakespeare and his contemporaries—problems of genre, of character, of plot construction—in an attempt to explain the success (or, sometimes, lack of success) of the major dramatists in "achieving form adequate to meaning" (23). Doran's unpretentious, readable study is justly famous as the first book on the aesthetics of Renaissance drama to understand the entire context, to perceive the Renaissance assumptions about dramatic art as a fusion of classical and medieval influences.

Editions and Reference Works 13

19. **Gurr, Andrew.** *Playgoing in Shakespeare's London.* 2nd edition. Cambridge: Cambridge Univ. Press, 1996.

Gurr focuses on the identity, class, and changing tastes of London playgoers from the opening of the Red Lion in 1567 to the closing of the theaters in 1642. He examines the locations, physical features, price scales, and repertories of the various playhouses, distinguishing particularly between "halls" and "amphitheatres" and rejecting the more common labels "private" and "public." Turning from the theaters, Gurr examines the playgoers, asking such questions as whether they ventured to the playhouses primarily to "hear" a text or to "see" a spectacle. In a final chapter, entitled "The evolution of tastes," he discusses assorted playgoing fashions: from the craze for Tarlton's clowning to the taste for pastoral and romance in the last years of Charles I. Two appendices list identifiable playgoers and references to playgoing during the time period.

20. **Gurr, Andrew.** *The Shakespearean Stage 1574–1642.* 3rd edition. Cambridge: Cambridge Univ. Press, 1992.

Gurr summarizes a vast amount of scholarship concerning the material conditions of Elizabethan, Jacobean, and Caroline theatrical production. Each of his six chapters provides a wealth of detailed information on theatrical life. The first gives an overview of the place of the theater in urban London from the 1570s until 1642, including an examination of the social status of playwrights, the differences and similarities between the repertories at the open-air amphitheaters (public) and at the indoor playhouses (private), and the changing role of court patronage of theater. Chapter two describes the typical composition of London theater companies and their regulation by the Crown. It also gives an historical account of the theatrical companies that at various times dominated the London theatrical scene. In his third chapter, Gurr looks at actors, discussing the famous clowns of the Elizabethan era, prominent tragic actors such as Burbage and Alleyn, and the repertory system within which they worked. The fourth chapter summarizes what is known about the playhouses, including information gleaned from the recent excavation of the remains of the Rose Theater, as well as accounts of the Globe Theater, The Fortune, the hall playhouses, and the Banqueting Hall. Chapter five discusses staging conventions and the differences between public and private theaters, and among the various particular theaters, in their use of song, music, clowning, and jigging. Also examined are stage properties and costumes. The final chapter analyzes information about audiences: who went to which kinds of playhouse and how they behaved. Gurr argues that women and all social classes were represented in theatrical audiences, with an increasing tendency in the seventeenth century for the private theaters to cater to a wealthier clientele who demanded a more sophisticated repertory with more new plays. This valuable book concludes with an appendix indicating at which playhouses and by which companies various plays were staged.

21. **Onions, C. T.** *A Shakespeare Glossary.* Oxford: Clarendon Press, 1911. 2nd edition revised, 1919. Repr., with corrections, 1946; with enlarged Addenda, 1958. Enlarged and revised by Robert D. Eagleson, 1986; corrected, 1988.

Onions's dictionary of Elizabethan vocabulary as it applies to Shakespeare was an offshoot of his work on the *Oxford English Dictionary*. Eagleson updates the third edition with new entries, using modern research (now aided by citations from the Riverside edition [see no. 2], keyed by the Spevack *Concordance* [see no. 24]), while conserving much from Onions's adaptation of *OED* entries to distinguish Shakespearean uses from those of his contemporaries and from modern standard meanings. The glossary covers only expressions that differ from modern usage, as with "cousin" or "noise." It includes some proper names with distinctive associations, such as "Machiavel," and explains unfamiliar stage directions: "sennet" (a trumpet signal). Many allusions are more fully elucidated, as with the origin of "hobby-horse" in morris dances, or the bearing of "wayward" on *Macbeth*'s "weird sisters." This text, which demonstrates the importance of historical awareness of language for accuracy in the close reading of Shakespeare, now has a brief bibliography of relevant texts but still lacks guidance about Elizabethan pronunciation.

22. **Rothwell, Kenneth S., and Annabelle Henkin Melzer.** *Shakespeare on Screen: An International Filmography and Videography.* New York: Neal-Schuman, 1990.

EDITIONS AND REFERENCE WORKS   15

This list of film and video versions of Shakespeare seeks to be comprehensive, covering the years 1899–1989, except that it excludes most silent films, referring the reader to Robert Hamilton Ball's *Shakespeare on Silent Film* (1968). It does include "modernizations, spinoffs, musical and dance versions, abridgements, travesties and excerpts" (x). The introduction, by Rothwell, offers an overview of screen versions of Shakespeare (1–17). The body of the work, with over 675 entries (21–316), is organized by play, listed alphabetically, and within each play chronologically. Represented are 37 plays and the *Sonnets*. *Pericles* and *Timon of Athens* appear only in the BBC versions in "The Shakespeare Plays" series. For *Hamlet* we have 87 entries. Included also are another 74 entries (317–35) for documentaries and other "unclassifiable" films and videos that present Shakespeare in some form, such as John Barton's "Playing Shakespeare" series and James Ivory's film, "Shakespeare Wallah." The sometimes quite extensive entries include information about and evaluation of the production, and an attempt to provide information about distribution and availability. The work concludes with a useful selected bibliography with brief annotations (337–45), a series of helpful indexes (349–98), and a list of the names and addresses of distributors, dealers, and archives (399–404).

23. **Schoenbaum, S.** *William Shakespeare: A Compact Documentary Life.* Oxford: Oxford Univ. Press, 1977. Repr., with corrections, 1978.

An abridged version of Schoenbaum's massive documentary study of Shakespeare published by Oxford in 1975, the *Compact Documentary Life* traces all textual evidence about Shakespeare chronologically from his grandfather's generation up to the deaths of Shakespeare's surviving family members. Legends for which there is no specific documentation—such as the deer-poaching incident—are examined for probability on the basis of surviving materials. Where appropriate, Schoenbaum juxtaposes biographical details with specific passages in Shakespeare's works. Amply illustrated and annotated, this work, unlike Schoenbaum's earlier, larger version and his later (1981) *William Shakespeare: Records and Images*, refers to documents but generally does not reprint them.

24. **Spevack, Marvin.** *The Harvard Concordance to Shakespeare.* Cambridge: Belknap Press of Harvard Univ. Press, 1973.

This text covers the total of 29,066 words (including proper names) used by Shakespeare in his plays and poems, in the modern-spelling text of *The Riverside Shakespeare* (see no. 2). Stage directions appear in another volume. Contexts are omitted for the first 43 words in order of frequency, mostly pronouns, prepositions, conjunctions, auxiliary verbs, and articles. Individual entries distinguish between prose and verse, and between total and relative frequencies. The modern spelling is not enforced with proper names or significant Elizabethan divergencies: "embassador-ambassador." While the cited context of each use is normally the line of text in which it appears, other limits occur when the sense requires further wording. This concordance helps to locate specific passages and also invites subtler research uses, such as study of the recurrence of words in each play: thus the continuity of *Henry VIII* from *Richard III* appears in their shared distinctive use of certain religious terms. Similarly, accumulated references show the divergence or consistency of meaning or associations for particular terms (Shakespeare's references to dogs are unfavorable). In using this text, one must remember that variant spellings or forms of speech may conceal recurrences of words with the same root or meaning (guilt, gilt, guilts, guilty, guiltily, guiltless), while similar spellings of the same word may have contrasting senses (your grace [the Duke] of York, the grace of God, external grace). The contexts provided ensure awareness of most complications, but rarely provide the complete syntactical setting required for exact interpretation of a word. The magnitude of the effort involved in this concordance indicates the research gain from electronic procedures, which also permit many permutations of its data, as seen in the eight volumes of Spevack's *A Complete and Systematic Concordance to the Works of Shakespeare* (1968–70).

25. **Styan, J. L.** *Shakespeare's Stagecraft.* Cambridge: Cambridge Univ. Press, 1967. Repr., with corrections, 1971.

Styan's book explores how Shakespeare's plays would have worked, theatrically, on the Elizabethan stage. Beginning with a discussion of the kind of stage for which Shakespeare wrote and of the conventions of performance that obtained on that stage, Styan then devotes the bulk of his attention to Shakespeare's handling of the visual and aural dimensions of performance. He argues that the scripts guide actors in communicating aurally, visually, and kinetically with an audience. Topics considered include gesture, entrances and exits, the use of downstage and upstage playing areas, eavesdropping encounters, the visual orchestration of scenes involving one or several or many characters, the manipulation of rhythm and tempo, and variations among stage voices. The final chapter, "Total Theater," discusses the inseparability of all the elements of Shakespeare's stagecraft in the shaping of a theatrical event aimed at provoking and engaging the audience's fullest response. The book makes a strong case for studying Shakespeare's plays as flexible blueprints for performance that skillfully utilize and transform the stagecraft conventions of the Elizabethan theater.

26. **Wells, Stanley, ed.** *The Cambridge Companion to Shakespeare Studies.* Cambridge: Cambridge Univ. Press, 1986. Repr., 1991.

Wells has assembled 19 other scholars to write on different aspects of Shakespeare studies; most of the essays include endnotes and a reading list. S. Schoenbaum writes about Shakespeare's life (chap. 1), W. R. Elton places him in the context of the thought of his age (chap. 2), Peter Thomson discusses contemporaneous playhouses and actors (chap. 5), and Alan C. Dessen places Shakespeare in the context of his age's theater conventions (chap. 6). Essays more on Shakespeare's writing are Robert Ellrodt's on the nondramatic poetry (chap. 3), Inga-Stina Ewbank's on his use of the arts of language (chap. 4), and the pairing of David Daniell's on the traditions of comedy (chap. 7) and G. K. Hunter's on the traditions of tragedy (chap. 8). R. L. Smallwood focuses on the ten plays about English history (chap. 9). MacD. P. Jackson discusses canonical and textual questions (chap. 10). The last chapters cover stage history and the history of literary criticism. Russell Jackson reviews stage history from 1660 to 1900 (chap. 11), Roger Warren carries this review into the twentieth century (chap. 14), and Robert Hapgood extends the coverage to film and television (chap. 15). Harry Levin surveys the dominant critical approaches from 1660 to 1904 (chap. 12), and in chap. 13 three scholars discuss twentieth-century trends in the study of the comedies (Lawrence Danson), tragedies (Kenneth Muir), and histories (Edward Berry). Terence Hawkes defines some of the newer critical approaches (chap. 16), and Dieter Mehl concludes the volume with a discursive list of important Shakespearean reference books (chap. 17). This book replaces the earlier *A New Companion to Shakespeare Studies* edited by S. Schoenbaum and K. Muir in 1971.

NOTE ON BIBLIOGRAPHIES

In addition to the above works, readers should be aware of the various bibliographies of Shakespeare studies. Among the most valuable are Stanley Wells, *Shakespeare: A Bibliographical Guide*, Oxford: Clarendon Press, 1990; David M. Bergeron and Geraldo U. De Sousa, *Shakespeare: A Study and Research Guide*, 3rd edition, Lawrence: Univ. Press of Kansas, 1995; Larry S. Champion, *The Essential Shakespeare: An Annotated Bibliography of Major Modern Studies*, 2nd edition, New York: Hall, 1993. Thorough bibliographies for each of a gradually increasing number of plays have been appearing since 1980 in the Garland Shakespeare Bibliographies, general editor William L. Godshalk. An important specialized bibliography is John W. Velz, *Shakespeare and the Classical Tradition: A Critical Guide to Commentary, 1660–1960*, Minneapolis: Univ. of Minnesota Press, 1968. In the special area of Shakespearean pedagogy, a useful (although brief) bibliography appears in Peggy O'Brien, "'And Gladly Teach': Books, Articles, and a Bibliography on the Teaching of Shakespeare," *Shakespeare Quarterly* 46 (1995): 165–72. For information on new materials on the study of Shakespeare, readers should consult the annual bibliographies published by *Shakespeare Quarterly* (*World Shakespeare Bibliography*), *PMLA* (*The MLA International Bibliography*, also available on-line and on CD ROM), the Modern Humanities Research Association (*Annual Bibliography of English Language and Literature*, available on-line), and the English Association (*The Year's Work in English Studies*). Ph.D. theses on Shakespeare are listed in *Dissertation Abstracts International*, which is also available on-line.

II. SHAKESPEARE AND THE RENAISSANCE STAGE TO 1616

A. General Studies of the Elizabethan Theatre

27. **Armstrong, William A.** *The Elizabethan Private Theatres: Facts and Problems.* London: Society for Theatre Research, Pamphlet Series 6, 1958.

This pamphlet reviews the prices, audiences, stages, and actors in the indoor "private" theatres of Renaissance London. It stresses their more elite, restrained, and sophisticated character. Armstrong notes contemporary allusions to lighting, length of performance, the use of sets, props, curtains, and upper and lower stages. This overview establishes major considerations relevant to Shakespeare's use of the Blackfriars Theatre. For Armstrong's more detailed study of audience characteristics in contemporary texts, see "The Audiences of the Elizabethan Private Theatres." *Review of English Studies* 10 (1959): 234–49.

28. **Barish, Jonas.** *The Antitheatrical Prejudice.* Berkeley: Univ. of California Press, 1981.

Barish reviews hostility to the theatre from Plato to the present. While the book stresses such moderns as Rousseau and Nietzsche, it also deals with the Renaissance theatre: Puritans, following St. Augustine, attacked the theatres until they closed them in 1642. Their views are explained in Chapter IV: Puritans and Proteans (80–131), and Chapter VI: Puritans, Popery, and Parade (155–90). Barish explains their arguments as censure of acting by its correlation with mimicry, falsification, disguise, and transvestism; its association with exhibitionism, indecorum, impropriety, subversion, and

Papism; and its use of scandalous themes and plots. In Chapter V: Jonson and the Loathèd Stage (132–54), Barish uses Ben Jonson to represent the anti-populist neoclassicism of Shakespeare's period. He shows that Romantics' substitution of imaginative reading for stage performance recurs in Yvor Winters, Harry Berger, and the New Critics; and that "sincerity" in Puritans and Romantics anticipates the subjective acting techniques of Stanislavsky and The Method.

29. **Baskervill, C. R.** "The Custom of Sitting on the Elizabethan Stage." *Modern Philology* 8 (1911): 581–89.

This article argues for an earlier date than 1597 for audience members sitting on the stage, listing references to show the practice occurred in both public and private theatres at least a few years earlier, despite frequent objections from theatre professionals. It shows that the practice was not necessarily limited to the later private theatres like Blackfriars. Its conclusions have been confirmed by Gabriel Egan, "The Situation of the 'Lords' Room': a Revaluation." *Review of English Studies* 48 (1972): 297–309. Egan records complaints suggesting that the view from the Lords' Rooms in the first galleries on either side of the stage was blocked by spectators seated on the stage, from as early as 1576 to as late as 1642.

30. **Bentley, Gerald Eades.** *The Profession of Dramatist in Shakespeare's Time 1590–1642.* Princeton: Princeton University Press, 1971. Repr. (corrected) as a single paperback with next entry, 1986.

Bentley reviews the professional circumstances affecting London playwrights in the Renaissance. This book surveys identifiable dramatists; their status and that of the theatre; and relations within acting companies (pay, contracts, regulation, and censorship). Sections cover collaboration, revision, and publication. The text cites precise details and illustrations often only indirectly related to Shakespeare, but suggesting his working conditions.

31. **Bentley, Gerald Eades.** *The Profession of Player in Shakespeare's Time 1590–1642.* Princeton: Princeton Univ. Press, 1971. Repr. with previous entry in a single paperback, 1986.

Bentley outlines the working conditions of Renaissance actors, discussing companies, apprentices, hired men, sharers, managers, touring outside London, and casting (from cast-lists in printed quartos and manuscripts). The book gives precise data about the practical activities and personalities of theatre staffs. Shakespeare rarely appears in the text, but it relates to his close associates, and the comments on casting and doubling, and on boy-actors, are relevant.

32. **Bergeron, David M.,** *English Civic Pageantry, 1558–1642.* London: Edward Arnold, 1971.

Bergeron reviews the types and procedures of royal pageants under Elizabeth I, James I, and Charles I, then progresses to the pageant-work of London dramatists. While Shakespeare appears indirectly, Bergeron shows that the pageant form establishes many images, attitudes, and concepts found in such history plays as *Richard II*. He suggests that Shakespeare may have derived these effects from his observations of such occasions as Queen Elizabeth's 1575 visit to Kenilworth, which anticipated Shakespeare's depictions of pageantry. Bergeron relates the form to mythological allusions of Shakespeare's earliest and latest plays, and he shows how the pageants establish a visual and symbolic context for English Renaissance drama.

33. **Bevington, David.** *From Mankind to Marlowe: Growth and Structure in the Popular Drama in Tudor England.* Cambridge: Harvard Univ. Press, 1962.

Bevington demonstrates Elizabethan theatre's structural and thematic heritage from medieval popular drama, stressing non-humanists like Skelton and Bale, the moralities, chronicle plays, romance, and homiletic tragedy. He covers repertory, casting, doubling and actors' versatility, the limits of structure and staging of plays, and of casts. These characteristics are linked to Marlowe's major plays, where realism and secularism exist in tension with traditional moral concerns. The medieval traditions apply to Elizabethan drama generally, as shown by Bevington's allusions to Shakespeare: he detects debts to traditional Vice figures in Richard III, Falstaff, and Iago. Most of the other medieval practices, allegorical, didactic, and theatrical, which are reviewed in this book could also be applied to interpretation of many Shakespearean plays. An Appendix reprints cast lists of relevant "Plays 'Offered for Acting'" (263–71) up to 1603.

34. **Bradbrook, Muriel.** *The Rise of the Common Player: a Study of Actor and Society in Shakespeare's England.* London: Chatto and Windus, 1962.

This book consolidates earlier work by Chambers and Greg (nos. 16, 45). Part 1, on "Players and Society," covers the social history of the public theatres from Chaucer to Elizabeth I, with the evolution from minstrel to academic and professional actors. Part 2 reviews "Common Players, 1573–1600," stressing individual actors such as Laneham, Tarlton, and Alleyn. Part 3 surveys "Household Players, 1574–1606" both clerical and secular, with the boys' companies. Part 4 explores drama's role in society: royal welcomes and private entertainments, and institutional (usually collegiate) revels at Christmas, etc. The book is not original but comprehensive, covering not just social issues but artistic ones: genres, influences, and analogues.

35. **Bradley, David.** *From Text to Performance in the Elizabethan Theatre: Preparing the Play for the Stage.* Cambridge: Cambridge Univ. Press, 1992.

Bradley explores Elizabethan performances via documents reflecting scripts' preparation for the stage, mostly lesser Elizabethan plays: their prompt-books, cast lists, and plot summaries for audiences. Surviving data is fragmentary, but he interprets scene structure and sequences through notations of entrances and exits. He links cast-size to probable doubling and costuming, which might affect interpretation, particularly when stage directions about them are added to the script. An Appendix cites known performances, 1497 to 1625, with authors, titles, and companies; dates of performance, registration, and publication; maximum, minimum, and probable cast numbers, men and boys; and number of lines. The discussion is technical, with important details about procedures and concerns in preparing Elizabethan scripts for staging. While the book notes that only one of the surviving Elizabethan plot summaries applies to a Shakespeare play (*Troilus*), its account of Elizabethan theatrical practices applies to all his work.

36. **Cook, Anne Jennalie.** *The Privileged Playgoers of Shakespeare's London, 1576–1642.* Princeton: Princeton Univ. Press, 1981.

Cook cites contemporary data suggesting greater dominance of London's playhouses by the city's privileged classes than documented by earlier scholars as in A. Harbage, *Shakespeare's Audience* (New York, 1941). Cook argues that privileged classes were the most consistent patrons of all types of theatre, ensuring "an intelligent audience" requiring "complex philosophical, theological or aesthetic ideas" (273–74). While she validates upper-class participation in theatre audiences and illuminates their behavior, her lack of data on other classes does not prove their absence or lack of influence. Cook's emphasis on the upper-class has been countered by Andrew Gurr's demonstration (no. 19) of the presence of a cross-section of English society in the Elizabethan theatres, thus reconfirming Harbage's account.

36a. **Cox, John D., and David Scott Kastan, eds.** *A New History of Early English Drama.* New York: Columbia Univ. Press, 1997.

This anthology consolidates into a single volume the work of many scholars listed in other entries of this bibliography. The essays most relevant to Shakespeare performance during his lifetime are Alan H. Nelson, "The Universities: Early Staging in Cambridge"; John R. Elliott, Jr., "Early Staging in Oxford"; Anne Higgins, "Streets and Markets"; John Orrell, "The Theaters"; Paul W. White, "Theater and Religious Culture"; Gordon Kipling, "Wonderful Spectacles: Theater and Civic Culture"; Diana E. Henderson, "The Theater and Domestic Culture"; Graham Parry, "Entertainments at Court"; Barbara A. Mowat, "The Theater and Literary Culture"; Michael D. Bristol, "Theater and Popular Culture"; Jean MacIntyre, Garrett P. J. Epp, "'Cloathes worth all the rest': Costumes and Properties"; Richard Dutton, "Censorship"; Ann J. Cook, "Audiences: Investigation, Interpretation, Invention"; Peter Thomson, "Rogues and Rhetoricians: Acting Styles in Early English Drama"; W. R. Streitberger, "Personnel and Professionalization"; Jeffrey Masten, "Playwrighting: Authorship and Collaboration"; Peter W. M.

Blayney, "The Publication of Playbooks"; Kathleen E. McLuskie, Felicity Dunsworth, "Patronage and the Economics of Theater"; Eric Rasmussen, "The Revision of Scripts"; Roslyn L. Knutson, "The Repertory"; Paul Werstine, "Plays in Manuscript." There are a bibliography, general index, and index of plays. Material in this anthology is covered in expanded form in items listed elsewhere in this bibliography under the above authors' names (see author index).

37. **Dessen, Alan C.** *Elizabethan Drama and the Viewer's Eye.* Chapel Hill: Univ. of North Carolina Press, 1977.

Dessen investigates the effects of drama on audiences from the viewpoint of both theatergoers and scholars. He begins with practices in the later morality plays. Then he shows how scenic details recur in sequences of scenes inviting comparison, such as the allusion to Pyrrhus killing Priam, which prefigures Hamlet's treatment of Claudius. He argues that recurring images such as Hal's manipulation of Francis heighten awareness of previous manipulations of Hotspur in *1 Henry IV*. There is also investigation of the critical effect of discrepancy between an audience's perceptions and those of stage characters, as in the deceptions of Beatrice and Benedick, and of Malvolio. He stresses the discrepancy between Gloucester's understanding of his fall from the cliff in *King Lear* and the audience's perception that it did not happen as Gloucester believes it did. Dessen traces the implications of symbolic action (the descent of Richard II at Berkeley Castle) and staged psychomachia (the symbolic "madness" of Malvolio in *Twelfth Night*). The book explores symbolic Elizabethan stage practices to provide a plausible context for audience responses to some less realistic modern Shakespeare productions.

38. **Dessen, Alan C.** *Elizabethan Stage Conventions and Modern Interpreters.* Cambridge: Cambridge Univ. Press, 1984.

Dessen expounds Elizabethan stage conventions through textual clues in Renaissance drama and through modern interpretations, both scholarly and theatrical. He reviews details such as the validity of the quarto stage direction for the Nurse to snatch Romeo's dagger when "he offers to stab himself" (3.3). He also treats soliloquies both in Elizabethan convention and in modern verisimilitude; symbolic meaning and realistic considerations in staging battles and fights; offstage "unstageable" events; the symbolism of loose-haired wigs in female madness; and how gestures, props, and costumes suggest locations such as night scenes, which modern lighting control often makes too dark to see such details which were fully visible on the daylit Elizabethan stages. Some of his interpretations of stage business are convincing, others only suggestive. The larger Elizabethan context for Shakespeare staging is explored in T. W. Craik, "The Reconstruction of Stage Action from Early Dramatic Texts." *Elizabethan Theatre* 5 (1975): 76–91. See also A. Drew-Bear, *Painted Faces on the Renaissance Stage: the Moral Significance of Face-Painting Conventions* (1994).

39. **Dutton, Richard.** *Mastering the Revels: the Regulation and Censorship of English Renaissance Drama.* Iowa City: Univ. of Iowa Press, 1991.

This book explains how the Renaissance English dramatists were reviewed, controlled, and even punished by the authorities, led by the Master of the Revels. Dutton argues that this control has been overstressed by New Historicists and Cultural Materialists anxious to explore repression and subversion, while he feels that operations were less severe, as authorities often avoided confrontation, even with Marlowe's provocative writings. This study concerns English drama from 1581 to 1626, and suggests that Shakespeare rarely ran into difficulties, despite two noted occasions: over the use of the Protestant martyr Sir John Oldcastle as a model for the character later renamed Sir John Falstaff (102–7), and over the restaging of *Richard II*'s deposition scene as a precedent for Essex's attempt to dethrone the aging Elizabeth I (117–27). Dutton delimits the pressures dramatists like Shakespeare may have felt in composition. See also J. Clare, *"Art made tongue-tied by authority": Elizabethan and Jacobean Dramatic Censorship* (1990).

40. **Eccles, Mark.** "Elizabethan Actors 1: A-D." *Notes & Queries* 236, n.s. 36 (1991), 38–49. "Elizabethan Actors II: E-J." *Notes & Queries* 236, n.s. 36 (1991), 454–61. "Elizabethan Actors III: K-R." *Notes & Queries* 237, n.s. 37 (1992), 293–303. In progress.

Eccles adds many significant new facts to the biographical data about actors mentioned in Bentley and Chambers (nos. 14, 16), as well as E. Nungezer, *A Dictionary of Actors and of Other Persons Associated with the Public Representation of Plays in England before 1642* (1929). The alphabetical survey is not yet complete, as listed.

41. **Feuillerat, Albert.** *Documents Relating to the Office of the Revels in the Time of Queen Elizabeth.* Louvain: A. Uystpruyst, 1908.

Part I reviews documents about the Office and Officers of the Revels. Part II provides extracts from 1558 through 1601. There is a chronological list of plays mentioned, with 50 pages of notes and three indexes. This text is a useful primary source for Elizabethan theatrical data.

42. **Foakes, Reginald A.** "The Player's Passion: Some Notes on Elizabethan Psychology and Acting." *Essays and Studies,* New Series, 7 (1954): 62–77.

Foakes stresses the relevance of the Elizabethan psychology of Timothy Bright, taking a middle position about Elizabethan acting, which he sees as ranging from "natural" to "formal." He investigates Elizabethan character types, psychosomatic correlations, and conventions of behavior in such matters as love. He explores such sources as puritan critics of the theatre like Gosson (no. 44), apologists for it such as Thomas Heywood (no. 50), critiques of actors, and other sources concerning boy actors as parodists of professional actors. He argues that Elizabethan acting extended to extremes of passion and action that are now likely to seem forced or grotesque but that still fall within the modern range of what seems realistic and were "thought at the time to be lifelike" (76). In this he takes a middle position between the rhetorical formalism which A. Harbage sees as intrinsic to the acting style in English Renaissance theatres, in "Elizabethan Acting." *PMLA* 54 (1939): 685–708, and the more naturalistic vein attributed to Elizabethan actors by M. Rosenberg, in "Elizabethan Actors: Men or Marionettes?" *PMLA* 69 (1954): 915–27. Harbage had been supported earlier by L. L. Marker, in "Nature and Decorum in the Theory of Elizabethan Acting," *Elizabethan Theatre* 2 (1970): 87–107. See also J. L. Donawerth, "Shakespeare and Acting Theory in the

English Renaissance." In *Shakespeare and the Arts*, ed. C. W. Cary and H. S. Limouze, 165–78 (1982).

43. **Foakes, Reginald A.** "Playhouses and Players." In *The Cambridge Companion to English Renaissance Drama*, ed. Albert R. Braunmuller and Michael Hattaway, 1–52. Cambridge: Cambridge Univ. Press, 1990.

Foakes gives a current overview of the English Renaissance theatre, with illustrations, plans, and maps, reflecting recent discoveries. The essay covers the early private playhouses, the later theatres, players and playing, and includes a current bibliography. Among theatres Foakes discusses are Blackfriars, Boar's Head, Bull, Cockpit/Phoenix, Curtain, Fortune, Globe, Hope, Newington Butts, Paul's, Porter's Hall, Red Bull, Red Lion, Rose, Salisbury Court, Swan, Theatre, and Whitefriars. As well as other aspects of theatre layout and use, Foakes explores the structure of the stage facade provided by the tyring house in such theatres. Among the players' companies he mentions are the King's Men, the Lord Admiral's Men, the Lord Chamberlain's Men, and the Queen's Men. Foakes considers these companies' use of boy actors such as Nathan Field, and clowns such as Richard Tarlton, as well as of leading actors such as Edward Alleyn and Richard Burbage. This substantial essay establishes current knowledge in the field. A recent collection of essays with coverage such as this one and its source has been edited by J. D. Cox and D. Kastan, *A New History of Early English Drama* (1997): no. 36a.

44. **Gosson, Stephen.** *The School of Abuse, Containing a Pleasant Invective Against Poets, Pipers, Players, Jesters, etc.* London: 1579; repr. London: Shakespeare Association, 1891.

This treatise, by the failed playwright Gosson, is a Puritan denunciation affording observations of staging and audience behavior as he attacks degenerate Elizabethan manners via the theatre. He censures the evil examples favored in the plots and characters of contemporary drama, and he censures the transvestism in the theatre's use of exclusively male actors, illustrating contemporary attitudes towards gender. He attacks the feigning involved in professional acting as a dangerous precedent for insincerity and hypocrisy. Gosson alludes to such formal matters as the use of act and scene divisions. He distinguishes between the wickedness of seeing contemporary plays performed, and the propriety of private reading of more virtuous scripts.

45. **Greg, Walter W., ed.** *Dramatic Documents from the Elizabethan Play-houses: Stage Plots; Actors' Parts; Prompt Books.* 2 vols. Oxford: Clarendon Press, 1931.

Greg surveys documentation from extant Elizabethan sources about the practices of the Elizabethan theatres. He includes facsimiles and transcripts of, and commentary on, eight extant dramatic plots (single-sheet summaries of a play's story for the convenience of the audience); the actor's part for the role of Orlando (a single actor's script excerpted, as was customary, from Greene's play *Orlando Furioso*); and select pages from nine prompt books of the Elizabethan period, with commentary. The section on surviving actor lists cites data on actors mentioned by name. There is also a descriptive list of surviving manuscript plays. Greg's material provides primary, detailed information about the operation of Elizabethan theatres, relevant to the working conditions for a dramatist and actor such as Shakespeare.

46. **Gurr, Andrew.** *The Shakespearian Playing Companies.* Oxford: Clarendon Press, 1996.

Gurr surveys the history of the London theatre companies from 1560 to 1642. The first section provides an historical overview of the social and political contexts of the companies. The second part narrates the history of individual companies, including sections on Strange's/Derby's Men, 1564–1620, and Pembroke's Men, 1591–1601; Hunsdon's/Chamberlain's/King's Men, 1594–1608; King's Men, 1608–1642. The book consolidates, in a deft and intelligible form, the vastly increased information uncovered by research since E. K. Chambers, no. 16. See also Gurr's other major studies (nos. 19 and 20).

47. **Hart, Alfred.** "The Time Allotted for Representation of Elizabethan and Jacobean Plays." *Review of English Studies* 8 (1932): 395–413.

Hart here interprets the elaborate tables of data in the first part of his argument: "The Length of Elizabethan and Jacobean Plays," *Review of English Studies* 8 (1932): 139–54. He asserts that Shakespearean performances lasted about two hours, excluding introductory and concluding music, and that the dramatist expected scripts to be cut to about 3,000 lines. He distinguishes between shorter reading time and time for full performance, but thinks Elizabethan actors spoke faster than modern ones. Though printed texts might average 2,490 lines, he estimates (407) that less than 2,400 lines in typical performance scripts might run for up to two and a quarter hours, allowing time (starting at 2 p.m.) for audiences to get home by dark most of the year. He lists time references in scripts and other documents.

48. **Hattaway, Michael.** *Elizabethan Popular Theatre: Plays in Performance.* London: Routledge & Kegan Paul, 1982.

The first part of this overview of Elizabethan performance uses contemporary material (mostly scripts) to illustrate the major practical factors: theatres and stages, performances, players and acting. The second part illustrates the operation of these resources by accounts of how five distinctive plays would have been performed (with analogies from modern productions of them): *The Spanish Tragedy* shows use of form; *Mucedorus,* meaning of convention; *Edward III,* the role of documentary data; *Dr. Faustus,* the use of ritual; and *Titus,* the effects of stylization. The book is a deft consolidation and application of established considerations about Elizabethan and modern productions.

49. **Henslowe, Philip.** *Henslowe's Diary: Edited with Supplementary Material, Introduction and Notes.* R. A. Foakes and R. T. Rickert, eds. Cambridge: Cambridge Univ. Press, 1961.

This is an exhaustive edition of Henslowe's records of his career as a producer of plays and as a theatre manager, which provide the best illustration of the business practices of the Elizabethan theatre in terms of available employment and building contracts, miscellaneous financial records, handling of physical properties, etc. The Introduction covers the history and character of the manuscript, with a detailed description, stating, "The main purpose of this edition is to make available again the text of the chief source for theatrical history between 1590 and 1604, Henslowe's Diary, and the fragments and manuscripts associated with it, in as convenient a form as possible" (ix). Indexes cover plays; names; a glossary; yearly dates. For further analysis see N. Carson, *A Companion to Henslowe's Diary* (1988). A facsimile of the difficult original handwritten text is available: *Henslowe's Papers: The Diary, Theatre Papers, and Bear Garden Papers*, ed. R. A. Foakes (1977).

50. **Heywood, Thomas.** *An Apology for Actors* (1612), ed. Richard H. Perkinson. New York: Scholars' Facsimiles and Reprints, 1941.

With the expertise of a Renaissance theatre-professional who wrote over two hundred scripts, Heywood offers elaborate defence of the theatre against puritanical censures such as Gosson's (see no. 44), providing much information about contemporary ideas and stage practices. Heywood argues for the antiquity, dignity, and moral worth of acting. He shows that such actors as Tarlton, Kempe, Sly, and Alleyn were greatly admired by aristocrats and even royalty. He provides anecdotal evidence of the ethical impact of performances on audiences, particularly when staged in a lively and lifelike way. He sees the theatre as a didactic agency able to enhance human values in society. He argues that the theatres increase London's attractiveness to foreigners while improving the language skills of natives. This edition includes the puritanical J[ohn] G[reene]'s *A Refutation of the Apology for Actors* (1615).

51. **Ingram, William.** *The Business of Playing: The Beginnings of Adult Professional Theater in Elizabethan London.* Ithaca: Cornell Univ. Press, 1992.

Ingram reviews legal documentation about the building and operation of three early theatres near London in 1576: the one at Newington Butts, the Theatre, and the Curtain. The concerns are legal and financial, without artistic references. The book explores contemporary historical theory, questioning most interpretations, before developing its key assumption that the most significant driving force of the enterprises is economic, if somewhat modified by social and political factors. The data present the economic context in which the physical structures of Elizabethan theatres evolved, through legal contracts, building costs, and other finances. Such material excludes the interest of the professional theatre personnel in aesthetics and interpretation. Following the current focus on "capitalist" financing of the Elizabethan theatre, the book omits other cultural factors in this theatre's emergence.

52. **Jewkes, Wilfred T.** *Act Division in Elizabethan and Jacobean Plays: 1583–1616.* Hamden, Conn.: Shoe String Press, 1958.

In Part 1, Jewkes reviews 236 printed plays to elicit the significance of division of about half these scripts into Acts, as seen, for instance, in the Shakespeare First Folio. Jewkes regrets that (as revalidated by Rowe), these divisions are still accepted despite their probable arbitrariness. In Part 2, Jewkes covers specific plays in detail, with a section (151–97) on Shakespeare. The argument is made that, unlike the private theatre scripts, regular printed texts added act divisions, so Shakespeare act-divisions were probably added for the Folio, rather than being intrinsic to the original scripts (other than the interventions by the Chorus in *Henry V, Romeo,* and *Pericles*). The book's detailed discussions question the nature of the breaks in performance, which Jewkes thinks most likely in scripts by newer writers performed after 1607 in private theatres. He indicates that the practice became normal by 1616.

53. **Joseph, Bertram L.** *Elizabethan Acting.* London: Oxford Univ. Press, 1951. Revised, 1964.

This book's second edition drops explanations of the function of rhetorical delivery in humanist learning and Elizabethan playscripts, and concentrates on physical aspects of stage acting, aided by Elizabethan comments on behavior offstage. Using such examples as *Romeo*, Joseph argues that Elizabethan acting involved natural behavior rather than formal, rhetorical performance. He asserts that in gesture and expression Elizabethans stressed feelings and motives, but included vocal recognition of the emotional and intellectual meanings of rhetorical devices (puns, repetitions, rhythms, rhymes, and other formulas) to express personality. As dramaturg, Joseph drew on Bulwer's plates of hand gestures in *Chironomia* (1644. Repr. John Bulwer, "*Chirologia*": *or the Natural Language of the Hand and "Chironomia": or the Art of Manual*

Rhetoric, ed. J. W. Cleary, 1974) to provide models when modern actors performed *Hamlet* and *Macbeth* at the Mermaid Theatre (1951–52). He finds that the Elizabethan actor's fusion of meaning, wit, and plausibility is best seen in Shakespeare. He believes that unique personality or individual eccentricity were less sought after by actors then than now. The book facilitates the reading of Shakespeare's works as scripts designed for specific stage interpretations.

54. **Lea, Kathleen Marguerite.** *Italian Popular Comedy: a Study in the Commedia dell' arte 1560–1620, with Special Reference to the English Stage.* 2 vols. Oxford: Clarendon Press, 1934.

Volume 1 covers a typical performance; the masks; the *scenarii*; antecedents and origins; and player companies. Volume 2 relates the *commedia* to the Elizabethan drama through discussion of Italian companies' visits to England and by overt allusions to specific masks and devices, including Shakespearean ones in *Errors, Merry Wives*, and *Tempest*. Appendices list Italian burlesque verse about *zanni* (buffoons); Italian plays connected to the *commedia*; performances in Venice listed by Sanudo; masks and actors in various records; *scenarii*, with extensive specimens; and a bibliography. While early and not exhaustive, this text provides a starting point for more detailed study of Shakespearean affinities with *commedia* such as the male/female reversals in *As You Like It* and *Twelfth Night* (II.179–82). Further Italian contexts are provided by L. G. Clubb, *Italian Drama in Shakespeare's Time* (1989), and by *Theatre of the English and Italian Renaissance*, ed. J. R. Mulryne, and M. Shewring (1991).

55. **Leggatt, Alexander, J. Leeds Barroll, Richard Hosley, and Alvin Kernan.** *Revels History of Drama in English, III. 1576–1613.* London: Methuen, 1975.

This volume in a series about theatre in English provides an illustrated review of Elizabethan and early Jacobean drama. It examines the period of Shakespeare's career in the theatre, with essays on the social and literary contexts, the companies and actors, the playhouses, the playwrights (including surveys of comedies, histories, and tragedies, with sections on Shakespeare). Later volumes in the series discuss the tradition of Shakespearean production. This volume is an encyclopedia of background material about performance of English Renaissance drama.

56. **Linthicum, M. C.** *Costume in the Drama of Shakespeare and His Contemporaries.* Oxford: Clarendon Press, 1936.

This compendium covers costume generally: colors and their symbolism; textiles (wool, linen, cotton, silk); trimmings (lace, embroidery, and ornaments); costumes (neckwear, sleeves, hats, shoes, accessories and fastenings, male and female garments). It provides a technical account of the production and significance of Elizabethan costume in drama and Shakespeare. The detail and comprehensiveness make this a valuable reference book for all aspects of costume in the period.

57. **Mehl, Dieter.** *The Elizabethan Dumb Show: the History of a Dramatic Convention.* Heidelberg, 1964. Trans. and revised, London: Methuen, 1965.

Mehl shows the evolution of dumbshows from pageant scenes with choric commentaries to preludes and abstractions of plays' themes (*Gorboduc*) to intrinsic parts of the action or themes (Kyd and the University Wits) until they become complex counterpoints with plays' totality (*Hamlet, Macbeth*, and later, Jacobean dramas such as Webster's). Mehl shows that, in the late plays, dumbshows may speed narrative (*Pericles*), or make moral points (*Tempest* and *Henry VIII*). Mehl demonstrates the different functions, meanings, and artistic implications of this minor, typically eclectic Elizabethan convention in six Shakespearean plays (the other is *A Midsummer Night's Dream*). They also appear in many others plays listed in an appendix.

58. **Morseberger, Robert E.** *Swordplay and the Elizabethan and Jacobean Stage.* Jacobean Drama Studies 37. Salzburg: Institut für Englische Sprache und Literatur, 1974.

After three chapters about fencing styles generally, Morseberger concentrates on actors' use of Elizabethan fencing techniques in stage fights and in the duel in *Hamlet*. He argues that such effects are often central in Shakespeare.

59. **Newton, Stella Mary.** *Renaissance Theatre Costume and the Sense of the Historic Past.* London: Rapp and Whiting, 1975.

Newton reviews the broad European context for Elizabethan drama in terms of costume, showing that efforts were made to achieve some historical plausibility of costume in plays set in earlier periods. This argument involves review of the theatres and their audiences, and allusions to contemporary art and to paintings in particular. The author raises issues of realism and referentiality in the arts, showing how these interacted with theatrical procedures. The book creates a conceptual frame for studying Elizabethan stage costuming.

60. **Shapiro, Michael.** "Annotated Bibliography on the Original Staging in Elizabethan Plays." *Research Opportunities in Renaissance Drama* 24 (1981): 23–49.

Shapiro's select critical bibliography covers structural features of the playing areas in London playhouses (public and private); staging techniques used in original productions of Elizabethan plays (acting, casting, and doubling; style and pacing; internal divisions; music and song; lighting; costumes and properties; and blocking). Each sub-section is prefaced by an introductory overview. This compendium is one of the few precedents for the present bibliography.

61. **Somerset, Alan.** "'How chances it they travel?' Provincial Touring, Playing Places, and the King's Men." *Shakespeare Survey* 47 (1994): 45–60.

Somerset cites evidence from municipal records, playscripts, and other contemporary documents to identify what were the reasons for Elizabethan theatre tours; the periods and hours for such provincial performances; the locations and playing spaces used; and the reception of such touring companies. He notes that tours were not solely governed by exigencies such as the closing of the London theatres because of plague. He identifies the rebuilt Guildhall in Leicester as one of the surviving locations, typical of such temporary performance spaces. He pursues the tour records both of Lord Leicester's company and of the Lord Chamberlain's Men, from 1594–1603, and from 1603 onwards those of the King's Men.

Though the book does not say which Shakespeare plays might be involved, its material relates to such possible touring scripts as the first quarto of *Richard III*.

62. **Stevens, David.** *English Renaissance Theatre History.* Boston: Hall, 1982.

This bibliography is set up chronologically with items alphabetized under year of publication, 1664–1979. Each entry's contents are summarized. The listings in the history of theatrical studies are more comprehensive than the cross-section in the present volume. The Index is focused on names rather than topics, so that scholarly development of specific issues cannot easily be pursued sequentially.

63. **Welsford, Enid.** *The Fool: His Social and Literary History.* London: Faber and Faber, 1935. Repr. 1966.

This detailed survey of the historical origins, professional role, and imaginative significance of the Court Fool in Europe includes a section about English examples, concluding with discussion of the Stage Clown. Shakespeare's Fools, including Falstaff, figure in the account, which shows Shakespeare's relationship to the precedents both in his conformity to and in his divergence from them. Welsford provides the context without exhausting interpretative options. For more recent interpretations, see R. B. Goldsmith, *Wise Fools in Shakespeare* (1958), and David Wiles, *Shakespeare's Clowns: Actor and Text in the Elizabethan Playhouse* (1987): nos. 96 and 124.

64. **Yates, Frances.** *Theatre of the World.* London: Routledge and Kegan Paul, 1969.

Yates uses John Dee and Robert Fludd to show the early influence of Vitruvius, before his use by Inigo Jones, arguing for neoclassical influence in the design of the Globe, seen in its very large stage, good acoustics, and painted ceiling of the stars of the Zodiac. Mrs. Thrales' report of seeing the Globe foundations in hexagonal form is used to argue for a Globe based on anticipations of Inigo Jones in an illustration from Fludd's *Art of Memory* (1619). Yates' theories still influence allegorical readings of the Elizabethan theatre in the stage decorations of the reconstructed Globe Theatre in

Southwark and the aesthetics of its operation by its artistic Director, Mark Rylance.

See also nos. 13, 14, 16, 19, 20, 26.

B. THE PHYSICAL CHARACTERISTICS OF ELIZABETHAN THEATRES

1. Background Studies

65. **Berry, Herbert.** *The Boar's Head Playhouse.* Illustrated by C. Walter Hodges. Washington, D.C.: Associated Univ. Presses for Folger Shakespeare Library, 1986.

Berry examines hitherto neglected contemporary documentation about one of the later conversions (1598) of an Elizabethan inn to a theatre, which staged plays contemporaneously with the Globe until 1616. Much of what survives covers legal issues during the theatre's earlier years and details the playhouse's physical structure rather than performances, but this adapted locale provides a foil to the operation of more popular and successful, purpose-built theatres such as the Globe.

66. **Campbell, Lily B.** *Scenes and Machines on the English Stage During the Renaissance.* Cambridge: Cambridge Univ. Press, 1923.

This is one of earliest investigations of how neoclassical influences and procedures spread to the Elizabethan theatre from Italy, via stage practices at the universities and the court. It discusses the evolution, from 1500 to 1700, of theatre scenery using perspective, with other, equally sophisticated, sound and visual effects. It leads to later research by John Orrell (no. 70) on how Vitruvius and Serlio influenced the court designers such as Inigo Jones, a trend which peaked in the Restoration practices of Davenant and Webb. Later scholarship uncovers more detail, but Campbell outlines the principal sources, and the role of Decorum and the Unities. More recent analysis appears in J. H. Astington, "Descent Machinery in the

Playhouse." *Medieval and Renaissance Drama in England* 2 (1985): 119–34.

67. **Foakes, Reginald A.** *Illustrations of the English Stage 1580–1642.* London: Scolar Press, 1985.

This annotated collection of 79 illustrations includes maps and panoramas, pictures relating to stages, printed illustrations in printed plays and other sources. It includes the known illustrations relevant to the Renaissance English theatres, with enlargements of significant details, each accompanied by analysis of their provenance, character, and significance. The book covers the setting and structure of the theatres, and the costuming and staging of scenes by actors, some identifiable. More material is gathered than in comparable texts, with a commentary skeptical of interpretative bias in established views.

68. **Hosley, Richard.** "The Origins of the So-called Elizabethan Multiple Stage." *The Drama Review* 12 (1968): 28–50.

Hosley mounts an attack on John Cranford Adam's concept of an Elizabethan multiple stage involving outer and inner stages, upper, balcony, and window stages—all considered to be distinct and fully developed playing spaces in *The Globe Playhouse: Its Design and Equipment* (1942). With many illustrations, Hosley argues that this diversity is unjustified and anachronistic. He argues for a primary, central playing space on Elizabethan stages, with a single major trap rather than the multiple traps postulated by Adams, as in modern stage-structure. Hosley's earlier arguments against Adams appeared in "Shakespeare's Use of a Gallery Over the Stage," *Shakespeare Survey* 10 (1957): 77–89; "The Gallery Over the Stage in the Public Playhouses of Shakespeare's Time," *Shakespeare Quarterly* 8 (1957): 15–31; and "The Discovery-space in Shakespeare's Globe." *Shakespeare Survey* 12 (1959): 35–46. Precedents for Hosley are provided by G. F. Reynolds, "Some Principles of Elizabethan Staging, I," *Modern Philology* 2 (1904): 581–614, and "Some Principles of Elizabethan Staging, II." *Modern Philology* 3 (1905): 69–97. Reynolds' views were further consolidated in *Staging of Elizabethan Plays at the Red Bull Theatre, 1605–1625* (1940).

69. **Nelson, Alan H.** *Early Cambridge Theatres: College, University and Town Stages 1464–1720.* Cambridge: Cambridge Univ. Press, 1994.

Nelson identifies precedents for London's public theatres found in the theatrically active University of Cambridge, from which came such leading Elizabethan playwrights as Greene and Marlowe. He draws on documentary evidence from the period, which he printed in the volume (1989) on the drama of Cambridge in the Toronto series of *Records of Early English Drama*. He concentrates on the use of college halls for performance, particularly Queens and Trinity, showing the unlikeliness of the use of college screens as a backing to any temporary stage since they constituted the main entrances to the college halls. See also A. Nelson, "Hall-Screens and Elizabethan Playhouses: Counter-Evidence from Cambridge," in *The Development of Shakespeare's Theatre*, ed. J. Astington (1992). Nelson challenges the concept of hall-screens as stage backing in R. Hosley, "The Origins of the Shakespearean Playhouse," *Shakespeare Quarterly* 15 (1964): 23–39. A broader coverage of academic drama appears in the essays edited by J. D. Cox and D. S. Kastan, *A New History of Early English Drama* (1997): no. 36a.

70. **Orrell, John.** *The Human Stage: English Theatre Design, 1567–1640.* Cambridge: Cambridge Univ. Press, 1988.

Orrell examines varieties of Renaissance theatres. Part I covers Festive Theatres, including early prototypes such as inns and beargardens, Henry VIII's Calais banqueting tent for the Field of the Cloth of Gold, as well as purpose-built theatres, which may not have evolved directly from their predecessors. He discusses emblems and decoration, including the canopy ceiling and lighting. He comments on Norden's views, the two Globe Theatres, and the Elizabethan Whitehall Banqueting Hall. Part II discusses Serlian theatres, which may reflect Elizabethan ideas of classical models, including that at Christchurch College, Oxford; the court theatres of Inigo Jones; and the private theatres at Blackfriars and the Cockpit/Phoenix in Drury Lane. Part III covers Serlian sets developed by Inigo Jones. The text reviews extant knowledge of English theatres of the period to provide a coherent interpretation of the evolution of English Renaissance stages. Precedents for Orrell's views appear in G. Kernodle, *From Art to Theatre: Form and Convention in the Renaissance* (1944).

71. **Stinson, James.** "Reconstructions of Elizabethan Public Playhouses." In *Studies in the Elizabethan Theatre,* ed. Charles Prouty, 55–124. Hamden, Conn.: Shoe String Press, 1961.

Stinson reviews the principal reconstructions of Elizabethan theatres, considering the work of Chambers, Hodges, Hosley, Smith, etc. (nos. 16, 68, 79, 84, etc.). The appendix lists the most cited London maps and views, with twelve plates of reconstructions, which are evaluated, with Hodges preferred as most cautious and conservative. This survey of the primary authorities in the field of studies of the Elizabethan theatre, and of their sources in basic materials from the Elizabethan period, provides a baseline against which to measure the assertions in the conjectures of later scholars.

72. **Wickham, Glynne.** *Early English Stages, 1300 to 1660.* London: Routledge and Kegan Paul, Vol. 1, 1959; Vol. 2, Parts 1 and 2, 1963, 1972.

The first two volumes of this continuing series are the most relevant: Volume 1 covers 1300 to 1576; Volume 2 covers 1576 to 1660. They discuss the evolution of English theatre in detail, with many illustrations, diagrams, appendices, and bibliographies. Among topics covered in the first volume are Shakespeare's precedents in indoor and outdoor entertainments in the Middle Ages; medieval dramatic theory and practice; players and commerce; and audiences and critics. The second volume discusses the Tudor regulation of the theatre which crushed the medieval tradition; the new stages; Reformation and Renaissance values, and state control; actors, playwrights, and the theatre; emblems and images; playhouses, stages, stage furniture, stage directions, etc. Wickham stresses later theatres' continuity with James Burbage's Theatre as emblematic in concept and not realistically representing actual locations. He sees expediency dominating design, with Elizabethan theatre structure determined by halls as well as inn-yards. He shows Inigo Jones establishing the new proscenium arch and painterly representation by

1605. This book is a convenient, if unfocused overview of the origins and development of English Renaissance theatres.

See also nos. 13, 14, 16, 19, 20, 25, 26, 27, 136, 156, 292.

2. Shakespeare's Theatres

73. **Adams, Joseph Quincy.** *Shakespearean Playhouses: A History of English Theatres from the Beginning to the Restoration.* Boston: Houghton Mifflin, 1917.

Adams provides documented histories for seventeen permanent English Renaissance playhouses and for five temporary or planned ones, as well as a chapter on early innyard theatres. He offers little about performances, but his comments and his extensive bibliography review earlier scholarship in the field of theatre operation and identify the basic references and relevant data for subsequent discussions.

74. **Berry, Herbert, ed.** *The First Public Playhouse: the Theatre in Shoreditch 1576–98.* Montreal: McGill-Queen's Univ. Press, 1979.

This anthology deals with the first custom-built public theatre in England. It includes essays by Glynne Wickham on "Heavens, Machinery and Pillars in the Theatre"; the editor's own "Aspects of Design and Use of the First Public Playhouse" and "Handlist of Documents about the Theatre"; Richard Hosley on "The Theatre and the Tradition of Playhouse Design"; and Oscar Brownstein on why Burbage found the Beargarden unsuited for theatrical leasing, because of its different audience considerations from the Theatre. The essays most relevant to Shakespeare are those which relate the Theatre to the Globe. Wickham argues that the Theatre did not have a canopy over the stage and that the addition of this with its lifting machinery allowed the Globe to surpass the Rose, which had exploited these resources previously. Hosley's essay demonstrates that the shaping of the timbers for use in constructing the Theatre would have required a similar structure for the new Globe, and even for the second Globe built on its foundations after the 1613 fire. Hosley believes that the Theatre already had a polygonal shape, three galleries with access by external stairs, and a covered stage, all with the exact dimensions of the later Globe built from its precut timbers, so that Shakespeare would have written throughout his career for a consistently structured theatre. Hosley argues that this design appeared in English architecture as early as the banqueting hall of Henry VIII at the Field of the Cloth of Gold near Calais in 1520. The book defines the contexts in which Shakespeare's theatre practices evolved. See also further background data in H. Berry, S*hakespeare's Playhouses* (1987).

75. **Blatherwick, Simon, and Andrew Gurr.** "Shakespeare's Factory: Archeological Evaluations from the Site of the Globe Theatre at 1/15 Anchor Terrace, Southwark Bridge, Southwark." *Antiquity* 66 (1992): 315–33.

This article reviews the data from the first, very limited excavations of the newly discovered site of the original Globe theatre and the second Globe. The authors show that the paucity of data leaves many matters conjectural and open to revision and to major development, if and when full exploration is permitted; but the material offered does tentatively begin the process of objectifying the structure of the original Globe Theatre and its successor. John Orrell provides an afterword (329–33) concluding that the Globe was probably a twenty-sided polygon with a diameter of 100 feet.

76. **Eccles, Christine.** *The Rose Theatre.* London: Hern Books, 1990.

Precipitated by the uncovering of the Rose Theatre's foundations, this illustrated book recapitulates the known history of Henslowe's Rose, 1587–1603, then reviews the nature and implications of the recent discoveries. The story involves many aspects of the theatrical scene in which Shakespeare's career began at the Rose and reached its apogee nearby. The book details the excavations and explores their archeological and artistic implications, concluding with an account of the subsequent inconclusive history of the site. See also *Documents of the Rose Playhouse,* ed. C. C. Rutter (1984).

77. **Gurr, Andrew, and John Orrell.** *Rebuilding Shakespeare's Globe.* New York: Routledge, 1989.

These scholars were involved in the reconstruction of the Globe

Theatre near its original site in Southwark. Chapters cover the origins and implementation of Sam Wanamaker's project; the audiences and operation of the original Globe Theatre; the physical structure of the first Globe and the Inigo Jones theatre design (the latter theatre has also been constructed on the modern Globe's site); and the detailed character of the modern development when completed. The book is illustrated from historical and modern sources covering Elizabethan precedents and designs for the project. Modifications of these studies, derived from actual experience in the restored Globe Theatre, appear in A. Gurr, "The Bare Island," *Shakespeare Survey* 47 (1994): 29–43; and A. Gurr, "Entrances and Hierarchy in the Globe Auditorium," *Shakespeare Bulletin* 14 (1996): 11–13. See no. 281.

78. **Hildy, Franklin J., ed.** *New Issues in the Reconstruction of Shakespeare's Theatre.* New York: Peter Lang, 1990.

This anthology of essays derives from an international conference at the University of Georgia (2/16–18/90) about the rebuilding of the Globe Theatre in Southwark, led by Sam Wanamaker. It includes an introduction about the project by the editor, followed by essays about the newly-discovered site of the Rose Theatre by Simon Blatherwick, Walter Hodges, John Orrell, and Andrew Gurr; and essays about the use of the rebuilt Globe by Alan Dessen, Hugh Richmond, and John Styan. The collection indicates some of the current developments stemming from the uncovering of the foundations of two of the original Southwark theatres, and the likely lines of development resulting from the opening of the first modern stage to recreate a structure like that of the Elizabethan public theatres. The collection represents work in progress, to be updated later.

79. **Hodges, C. Walter.** *The Globe Restored: A Study of the Elizabethan Theatre,* London: Oxford Univ. Press, 1953, 1968; repr. New York: Norton, 1973.

With many illustrations, Hodges attempts a detailed reconstruction of the original Globe Theatre from contemporary sources and parallels. He provides a substantial selection of primary materials from which to reconstruct the physical specifications of the first

Globe, with the aid of conjecture, including his own drawings and plans. With its line drawings, seventy-three plates, and seven appendices, the book provides a visual introduction to the relevant references and considerations in recreating Shakespeare's theatre, but recent research favors less elaborate speculation than his drawings reflect.

80. **Hodges, C. Walter.** *Shakespeare's Second Globe: The Missing Monument.* Oxford: Oxford Univ. Press, 1973.

Profusely illustrated by drawings and designs, Hodges' book reviews Hollar's drawings, discusses the second Globe Theatre's structure, roof, lantern, and interior, and then progresses to designs for a rebuilt Globe, with consideration of practical issues such as the design of the stage canopy. See also the accounts of plans to rebuild this theatre in *The Third Globe,* ed. C. W. Hodges, *et al.* (1980).

81. **Hotson, Leslie.** *Shakespeare's Wooden O.* London: Rupert Hart-Davies, 1959.

Hotson argues that Elizabethan stages preserved the medieval forms and procedures of pageants and theatre in the round, though the central position of most performance stages in Renaissance halls at court and in colleges permitted viewing from two sides of the stage, with curtained huts at either end of the stage for actors' entrances and exits. His argument is supported by documentation of performances in Spain, and at English universities and the royal court. He finds evidence that this format persisted in public theatres, including the Globe, where huts could have been two stories high and entered from a Green Room below the stage. He shows that aristocratic audiences were seated behind, above, and even at the rear of the stage. While he documents use of this format (King's College Chapel, 162; Queen's College, 172–73), his two lines of two-storied huts flanking the thrust stages of theatres such as the Globe would block the sightlines of many spectators, as his illustrations of key scenes show (27, 223). The idea of a below-stage Green Room also is unlikely, despite valid arguments on the spatial symbolism of diabolic entries from below-stage.

82. **Nagler, Alois M.** *Shakespeare's Stage.* Trans. Ralph Mannheim. New Haven: Yale Univ. Press, 1958. Revised, 1981.

Nagler starts by evoking a generic Elizabethan theatre via a brief overview of basic facts about Elizabethan theatres from the Theatre and Curtain on, from contemporary sources and from foreign analogues. He censures speculations by Adams, Hodges, and Hosley about inner and upper stages (nos. 68, 79, 80). He accepts tents and mansions, particularly in court performances. He considers Elizabethan acting and Shakespeare as director as well as the impact of the indoor Blackfriars theatre and contemporary masques. The book is brisk, well-informed, and challenging, but it argues overstrongly for use of tents, which seem too clumsy for fast moving action, and for use of the gallery, which is not confirmed by most scripts.

83. **Orrell, John.** *The Quest for Shakespeare's Globe.* Cambridge: Cambridge Univ. Press, 1983.

Orrell establishes the major dimensions of both of Shakespeare's Globe Theatres by analysis of the images of theatres in various townscapes of London from the period, particularly those of Wenceslaus Hollar. The argument depends on documentary techniques used in such compositions, leading to complex mathematical analysis of perspective. It is supported by discussion of Henslowe's contract for the Fortune Theatre. Orrell concludes from this evidence that the likely dimensions for both Globe Theatres are about 100 feet for the outside diameter, 70 feet diameter for the interior yard, containing a 49.5 feet wide stage, with a height of 32 feet to the eaves, and a gallery depth of 15.5 feet. Other issues addressed include a proposed number of twenty-four sides to the Globe's polygonal shape, and a stage orientation of 49 degrees east of north as the facing direction of the stage facade, close to sunrise at the summer solstice. Orrell's dimensions have been accounted overlarge in T. Fitzpatrick, "The Fortune Contract and Hollar's Original Drawing of Southwark: Some Indication of a Smaller First Globe," *Shakespeare Bulletin* 14 (1996): 5–10. So far London archeologists' investigation of the Globe's foundations since 1983 have not confirmed any of these calculations, but Orrell's procedures and sources remain illuminating.

84. **Smith, Irwin.** *Shakespeare's Blackfriars Playhouse: Its History and Its Design.* New York: New York University Press, 1964.

This exhaustive study covers Shakespeare's principal indoor theatre: previous history of the site and buildings, construction materials, first and second periods of theatrical use, physical characteristics of the theatre, script repertories, stage conventions. There are many illustrations and plans. The text establishes the exact physical conditions which Shakespeare had in mind when he wrote his later plays. The book provides a starting point for research involving the indoor theatre used by Shakespeare and about private theatre conditions in London in the early 17th century. See also R. Hosley, "A Reconstruction of the Second Blackfriars," *Elizabethan Theatre* 1 (1969): 74–88; and G. E. Bentley, "Shakespeare and the Blackfriars Theatre," *Shakespeare Survey* 1 (1948): 38–50. Bentley's view that this theatre's structure affected Shakespeare's dramaturgy is rejected by J. A. Lavin, "Shakespeare and the Second Blackfriars," *Elizabethan Theatre* 3 (1973): 66–81.

85. **Thomson, Peter.** *Shakespeare's Theatre.* London: Routledge and Kegan Paul, 1983. Revised 1992.

The first part of this book reviews and illustrates current knowledge about Shakespeare's company and its personnel; its theatre's structure and stage operation from 1599 to 1608; and its handling of scripts and of finances. The book stresses authentic contemporary references rather than the conjectures tending to dominate modern scholarship. Its factual survey establishes the information necessary for modern Shakespeareans to understand the basic procedures and resources involved in the day-to-day running of the company and how these would practically affect Shakespeare's theatre work. The second half of the book investigates the staging implications of three plays, through practical details of professional Elizabethan performances. Thomson chooses to examine *Twelfth Night* (music, props, locations in time and space), *Hamlet* (acting styles), and *Macbeth* (scene-by-scene staging analysis). The book's approach stresses performance procedures, constraints, and options, beginning with a reliable summary of modern research about Globe staging.

86. **Wilson, Jean.** *The Archeology of Shakespeare: The Material Legacy of Shakespeare's Theatre.* Stroud, U.K.: Allan Sutton Publishing, 1995.

Wilson provides a reassessment of the knowledge about the physical environment for the original performances of Shakespeare's plays resulting from the recent archeological discoveries at the sites of the Rose and Globe theatres. Her book extends beyond the excavations of the sites to setting them in the broader context of early Shakespearean performances through chapters on Shakespeare's life, on Elizabethan society and its broader theatrical aspects, and on the detailed operation of its various theaters, both open-air and indoors. A significant chapter consolidates the results and controversies arising from the excavations, including the establishment of dimensions for the Rose which were smaller than anticipated, as well as the discovery of modifications to enlarge the original size of that theater. Wilson's Globe material is more limited because of the premature termination of the excavations of that site, which prevented the drawing of conclusions. This book seeks to relate recent discoveries to the previously established historical context and to the professional practices at the Rose, Globe, and other Elizabethan theatres.

See also nos. 2, 13, 16, 19, 20, 25, 26, 36, 40, 45, 67, 70, 71, 72, 292, 293.

C. Shakespeare & Elizabethan Theatrical Practices

87. **Baldwin, Thomas W.** *The Organization and Personnel of the Shakespearean Company.* Princeton: Princeton Univ. Press, 1927.

Baldwin's encyclopedic survey examines the professional operations of the Elizabethan theatre which constituted the context for creation and performance of Shakespeare's plays, determining the technical skills, procedures, and behavior of the actors. Using both surviving documents and his own hypotheses, Baldwin outlines the relevant laws and procedures for company membership and the records of the individual actors involved; the roles of housekeepers and sharers; hired men; family relationships; finances and fees; actors and their specific roles in Shakespeare and Beaumont and Fletcher plays (determined through documents and from speculation). The book concludes with details of the bearing of these factors on Shakespeare's theatrical career, showing, for example, how type-casting affected characterization and thus influenced plot choices. Among many other items, some appendices cover the Admiral's Men to 1595; the finances of Shakespeare's company; assigned parts (in Beaumont, Fletcher, and Jonson as well as throughout Shakespeare); the estimated dates of Shakespeare's composition of his plays. This monumental study establishes most of the formative professional factors governing Shakespeare's theatrical career, particularly the identities of the individual actors and managers with whom he would have regularly worked throughout his career. Some of Baldwin's aesthetic assumptions and technical hypotheses may need adjustment in the light of recent scholarship and critical values.

88. **Berry, Ralph.** *Shakespeare and the Awareness of the Audience.* New York: St. Martin's Press; London: Macmillan, 1985.

Berry considers Shakespeare's skills in recognizing his performances' relation to the audience. He shows how *Richard III* first wins audience sympathy for its hero and then alienates its watchers, producing a distinctive catharsis. For Berry, *The Comedy of Errors* progresses (like the late romances) from existing tension to relaxing reconciliation. He feels *The Merchant of Venice* confronts the audience with its own prejudices. Berry finds that *Twelfth Night* dexterously blends sweetness and dryness, culminating in Malvolio's attack on a comic reading. For him, *Julius Caesar* creates audience revision of Roman society as a conservative ideal, while *Troilus and Cressida* subverts fashionable chivalry, and *Henry VIII* is a masque-like advocacy of royal prerogative. Berry raises valid issues that result from seeing audience impact as drama's primary goal, even if we may debate some of his exact specifications of outcomes. A similar approach has been applied to several comedies and *Hamlet* by M. W. Shurgot, *Stages of Play: Shakespeare's Theatrical Energies in Performance* (1998).

89. **Bevington, David.** *Action Is Eloquence: Shakespeare's Language of Gesture.* Cambridge: Harvard Univ. Press, 1984.

Bevington explores the "vocabulary of visual signals" (4) in Shakespeare's plays through stage directions and textual clues. Chapters cover 1) Visual Interpretation: realistic modes versus emblematic or allegorical ones in Elizabethan effects such as Lear's kneeling; 2) Costume and Hand-Props: letters as in *Love's Labour's Lost*, or rings and jewelry used for characterization as in *Merchant* and *Cymbeline*; 3) Language of Gesture and Expression: the physiology of weeping, anger, love; manners; hair-styles; changes of complexion; 4) Theatrical Space: the significance of parts of the stage as in Richard II's symbolic descent (3.3); 5) Ceremonies: the implications of marriages (often incomplete), coronations, punishments, executions, and common courtesies; 6) Maimed Rites in *Hamlet* as clues to theme and meaning. The book explores cues for physical expressions on stage to develop meaning and character.

90. **Bradbrook, Muriel.** *Elizabethan Stage Conventions: a Study of Their Place in the Interpretation of Shakespeare's Plays.* Cambridge: Cambridge Univ. Press, 1932. Repr., 1962.

Bradbrook shows how bare, open Elizabethan stages affect interpretation of Shakespeare's scripts and explain his flexibility. The book reviews the limitations of earlier criticism which attributed uniqueness to generic effects in Shakespeare by ignoring such factors. It shows the ways in which the poetry serves to replace the clues about time and place now offered by elaborate sets and properties. It also explores how characterization was affected by conventions such as soliloquy, and by the professional traits of the acting company. This brief study led the way for many fuller accounts (including her own numerous works in the field), but it still provides an overview of issues since approached more locally and technically.

91. **Brissenden, Alan.** *Shakespeare and the Dance.* Atlantic Highlands, N.J.: Humanities Press, 1981.

A dance critic, Brissenden uses dance manuals and other sources to show that dance was enjoyed by Elizabethans and accepted as a symbol of harmony. Brissenden argues that Shakespeare used this device to show order in a discordant world by dances in more than a dozen of his plays, and by allusions in thirty of them. This use is exemplified by the book's reference to many of the comedies, but particularly to *Love's Labour's, Dream,* and *Much Ado,* and to many tragedies, but most notably to *Romeo, Macbeth,* and *Timon.* He also shows that dances derived from contemporary masques occur in all the late plays, from *Pericles* to *Henry VIII.* The book stresses traditional choreography in Shakespeare, often neglected in modern productions, and invites debate.

92. **Davies, W. Robertson.** *Shakespeare's Boy Actors.* London: Dent, 1939. Repr., 1964.

Davies shows how scripts were adjusted for boy actors to make women's parts easier to act without artistic loss. He covers the shift from boys to actresses at the Restoration, discussing Elizabethan acting, puritan censures, and singing voices. Next follows play-by-play consideration of boys' technical skills in women's roles, with longer parts in comedies, usually formal, as in Portia's speech on mercy, and briefer, stylized passages in emotional or tender passages, for which audiences are carefully prepared. Despite early exceptions in *Henry VI* and *Richard III*, Davies finds women's parts for boys in histories and tragedies are fewer and briefer (Ophelia, Desdemona, Cordelia), with selective presentation of character (Cleopatra's sexuality is not fully staged). He argues that older, more aggressive women (Juliet's nurse, Volumnia, Paulina) were played by men; that indecent language was more acceptable with male actors as women; and that physical displays of affection, such as kisses and embraces, were accepted with boy actors. Davis antedates modern gender concerns, so that his detailed account of Shakespearean practices should be considered in the context of more recent general gender studies listed in no. 111a.

93. **De Bank, C.** *Shakespearean Stage Production: Then and Now.* New York: McGraw Hill, 1953.

This encyclopedic overview of the practical relationship of original forms of Shakespeare production to modern performances adapts Elizabethan practices to modern production procedures. Part 1 covers Elizabethan and modern treatments of staging, lighting, props, and sound effects. Part 2 relates Elizabethan acting to modern reconstructions. Part 3 discusses Elizabethan costume and modern versions. Part 4 describes Elizabethan music and dancing, including steps for the principal types of dance, and their role in the plays. There are detailed prescriptions for modern staging of specific scenes and exhaustive lists of items under the various topics above, with bibliographies. While directed to modern performers, these accounts provide basic data for all Shakespeare students.

94. **Dessen, Alan C.** *Recovering Shakespeare's Theatrical Vocabulary.* Cambridge: Cambridge Univ. Press, 1995.

Dessen reviews the stage directions, costuming, and props of about 600 scripts performed before 1642, in order to elicit the theatrical vocabulary relevant to the practices of Shakespeare and his contemporaries. Topics covered include the key metaphor in *Merchant*; Shakespeare's images; Elizabethan stage locales and modern interpretations; and Shakespearean use of italics. This work is a prelude to a dictionary of Elizabethan stage terminology.

95. **Flatter, Richard.** *Shakespeare's Producing Hand: A Study of his Marks of Expression to be found in the First Folio.* London: Heinemann, 1948. Retitled *Shakespeare's Theatrical Notation: A Study of his Marks of Expression to be found in the First Folio.* New York: Norton, 1948.

Flatter (a translator of Shakespeare into German) gives a close analysis of the Folio text to elicit possible business indicated by asides, entries, pauses, metrical gaps, irregular stresses, divided lines. He detects nuances in uses of "thou" or "you." He validates rhetorical punctuation for interpretation of tone and feeling. *Macbeth*'s text is used for application of such points, which may help performers of verse. Some of the arguments are affected by recent work on the First Folio (see Hinman, no. 4), but modern directors such as Patrick Tucker still find contemporary printings of Shakespeare illuminating, whether or not these may often reflect the intervention of scribes or compositors.

96. **Goldsmith, Robert B.** *Wise Fools in Shakespeare.* Liverpool: Liverpool Univ. Press, 1958.

Goldsmith's chapters treat The Fool of Tradition; Emergence of the Stage Fool; Elizabethan Fools and Clowns; Shakespeare's Wise Fools (Touchstone, Feste, Lavache, Lear's Fool); Critics in Motley (malcontents and satirists); The Fool in Fable (roles in comedy and tragedy). The book is more historical and critical in emphasis than about staging, but it sets Shakespeare's fools in context. See also C. S. Felver, *Robert Armin* (1961); and L. Hotson, *Shakespeare's Motley* (1952). See also no. 124.

97. **Gooch, Bryan N. S., and David Thatcher.** *A Shakespeare Music Catalogue.* 5 Vols. Oxford: Clarendon Press, 1991.

This encyclopedia covers over 20,000 compositions related to Shakespeare. Volumes 1, 2, and 3 identify music associated with the plays, set in alphabetical order, ending with the Sonnets, Poems and Commemorative Pieces, and Apocryphal Texts. Entries for each play begin with all Musical Stage Directions in the text (with commentators); then, Incidental Music (often with production details); Operas and Related Music; Non-Theatrical Vocal and Instrumental Music; Settings of Combined or Unidentified Texts; Obliquely Related Works; Non-Theatrical Vocal and Instrumental Music; and Non-Shakespearean Works. Entries for each composition include its composer, title, and opus number; manuscript data; title of composer's collection; city and date of publication, and publisher; form of work; vocal and instrumental specifications; names of librettists or translators; first performance data; cross-references; and repositories of printed texts. These lists often identify significant stage productions in detail (e.g., a neglected one of *The Two Noble Kinsmen*). Volume 4 contains indexes of Shakespeare titles and lines; the titles of musical works; the names of composers, arrangers, and editors; and the names of librettists and writers. Volume 5 contains a selected bibliography with sections on Theatre Music in Shakespeare's England; Shakespeare's Knowledge and Use of Music and Song; Shakespeare and Composers; Shakespeare and Musical Performance; Lists of Shakespeare Music; and Indexes of Shakespeare Titles, and of Proper Names. The work establishes a definitive account of a major aspect of Shakespeare performance, with much information of even broader significance. For more selective appreciation of music and Shakespeare see F. W. Sternfeld, *Music in Shakespearean Tragedy* (1963); P. J. Seng, *The Vocal Songs in the Plays of*

Shakespeare (1967); J. Scott Colley, "Music in the Elizabethan Private Theatres," *Yearbook of English Studies* 4 (1974): 62–69. See also J. H. Long's three studies, *Shakespeare's Use of Music: A Study of the Music and Its Performance in the Original Production of Seven Comedies* (1955); *Shakespeare's Use of Music: The Final Comedies* (1961); and *Shakespeare's Use of Music: The Histories and Tragedies* (1971).

98. **Graves, R. B.** "Elizabethan Lighting Effects and the Conventions of Indoor and Outdoor Theatrical Illumination." *Renaissance Drama,* New Series 12 (1981): 51–69.

Graves reviews indications of how night scenes were staged, including use of natural lighting in indoor theatres. He suggests that symbolic props were used rather than actual effects to brighten or darken the stage.

99. **Hapgood, Robert.** *Shakespeare: The Theatre-Poet.* Oxford: Clarendon Press, 1988.

For Hapgood, Shakespeare is a controlling dramatist, commenting on characters and action, as in the Chorus of *Henry V* in which an authorial point of view is vigorously established. Hapgood sees the role of playwright as sharing the kind of overt goals pursued by the casts in plays within plays such as *Hamlet*'s, but he also suggests that the dramatist restricts his actors' autonomy and recognizes the priority of the audience's interests, as in *Lear*'s exploratory testing of their resilience. Using modern performances, including film and video, Hapgood identifies Shakespeare's involvement in the plays' art and interpretation to restore his significant presence as a consciously controlling force in the effect of his plays.

100. **Hasler, Jörg.** *Shakespeare's Theatrical Notation: The Comedies.* Bern: Francke Verlag, 1974.

Hasler discusses visual and verbal imagery; theatrical notation (or performance instructions in the text) in major scenes (Shylock's trial, Hero's repudiation); parody (*Pyramus and Thisbe*); mirroring and overhearing; endings. While mostly critically interpretative, the book considers blocking and other staging factors, as with exactly how to perform the final words of *Love's Labour's Lost*.

101. **Holmes, Martin.** *Shakespeare and Burbage.* Totowa, N.J.: Rowman and Littlefield, 1978.

Holmes reconstructs the relationship of the stage talents of Richard Burbage to the texts of Shakespeare. Holmes correlates the increasing sophistication and naturalism of Shakespeare in his departure from his earlier rhetorical models for versification and verbal style (such as Marlowe acted by Alleyn) with the maturation of Burbage as an actor noted for his subtlety of pacing, tone, and cadence. While often conjectural, the study suggests how Shakespeare may have adapted his expression to the talents of his leading actor, showing that literary motivations in Shakespeare may be modified by practical factors in the theatre.

102. **Howard, Jean E.** *Shakespeare's Art of Orchestration: Stage Technique and Audience Response.* Urbana: Univ. of Illinois Press, 1984.

Howard applies affective criticism in the style of Stanley Fish to audience responses to Shakespearean performance, including responses that involve diverse sensory experiences: aural, physical, and kinetic. She notes how audience responses are cued by preparatory material (e.g., before Cordelia returns in Act IV of *Lear*). She also discusses the counterpoint of speeches interrupted by asides; the meaningfulness of unexpected silences; the bodily contrasts in public and private phases of *Hamlet*; the orchestration of structure, as in the use of crescendo in *1 Henry IV*; the alternation of restraint and release in *Twelfth Night*, used to illustrate all the earlier points. Audience reaction is taken to be Shakespeare's principal consideration in composing his plays.

103. **Jones, Emrys.** *Scenic Form in Shakespeare.* Oxford: Clarendon Press, 1971.

Concentrating on the tragedies and histories, Jones examines the dramatic structure of individual Shakespearean scenes and their progression, noting changes from sources and audience interaction. He looks at the scene as an individual unit, then as part of a sequence, considering the problem of *Othello*'s time-scheme and continuity. He defines the two-part structure of such plays. He displays the progression and growth of scenes within plays, but then expands this continuity on a larger scale from play to play. Focusing on key scenes, he examines *Lear*, censured as an episodic morality play. Scenes in *Macbeth* are related to *Henry VI, Richard III,* and *Caesar. Antony* is contrasted with *Henry V,* because it is written in beats rather than acts. Jones makes one aware of the importance of dramatic structure in the individual scenes, which he considers to be the basic units of Shakespeare's composition. Some precedents for Jones' approach appear in N. Coghill, *Shakespeare's Professional Skills* (1964), and M. Rose parallels some of Jones' materials and methods in *Shakespeare's Design* (1972). Recent analysis has expanded the dicussion, as in J. Hirsh, *The Structure of Shakespeare's Scenes* (1981).

104. **Kernan, Alvin.** *Shakespeare, the King's Playwright: Theater in the Stuart Court 1600–1613.* New Haven: Yale Univ. Press, 1995.

Kernan illustrates the effect on Shakespeare's art of his working for audiences at the Stuart court, with its distinctive social, political, and moral climate. Shakespeare's patron was King James I, but, while Kernan illustrates how this performance context affected Shakespeare's art and professional procedures, he argues that it did not reduce him to the role of either propagandist or secret subversive (see Montrose, no. 110). Kernan investigates how Shakespeare preserved his artistic integrity, while reviewing such complex questions as revenge and the royal succession in *Hamlet*; relations between royal prerogative and the law in *Measure*; the way Stuart lineage derived from Banquo in *Macbeth*; the divine right of kings in *Lear*; court decadence in *Antony*; the problems of archaic military aristocracy in *Coriolanus*; the role of art in *Tempest*. Kernan's appendix provides a calendar of the King's Men's court performances. Kernan demonstrates the interaction over moral, political, and artistic issues which would have occurred between the actors and their royal and courtly spectators during performances at court.

105. **King, T. J.** *Casting Shakespeare's Plays: London Actors and Their Roles 1590–1642.* Cambridge: Cambridge Univ. Press, 1992.

King surveys 52 scripts (the Folio, plus various Quartos) of 38 Shakespeare plays and finds that they require an average of ten men and four boys (for female parts) to perform them. The detailed study of normal expectations for doubling and tripling of parts is helpful, but much of the argument remains conjectural. Baldwin's ideas of type-casting (see no. 87) are also questioned in T. J. King, "The King's Men on Stage: Actors and Their Parts, 1611–32." *Elizabethan Theater* 9 (1986): 21–40.

106. **King, T. J.** *Shakespeare Staging 1599–1642.* Cambridge Mass.: Harvard Univ. Press, 1971.

King surveys 276 texts, mostly promptbooks, both manuscript and printed scripts with performance markings, and shows that these confirm the use of standard properties in front of a permanent set. Chapters (with lists and commentary on relevant plays) are headed "Above the Stage," "Doors or Hangings," and "Below the Stage." The book concludes with a re-creation, along the lines thus established, of the performance of *Twelfth Night* at the Middle Temple at Candlemas 1601/2. Appendix A. details recent scholarship, B. lists printed plays not included, and C. lists non-play dramatic texts. Primarily a reference work, this text offers a start in considering stage directions' implications in performance.

107. **Klein, David.** "Did Shakespeare Produce his own Plays?" *Modern Language Review* 57 (1962): 556–60.

Klein challenges Alfred Hart in *Modern Language Review* 36 (1941): 173–87, by offering evidence that Shakespeare did produce his own plays. The evidence is from a German traveler, Johannes Rhenanus, who observed a rehearsal, and by references in Dekker, Jonson, Marston, Massinger, Middleton, Munday, Nashe, and Rowley, showing that Elizabethan playwrights directed their own plays. The concept is redeployed in B. Hodgdon, "Shakespeare's Directorial Eye: a Look at the Early History Plays," in *Shakespeare's More Than Words Can Witness: Essays on Visual and Non-verbal Enactment in the Plays*, ed. S. Homan (1980). This argument also appears in J. Isaacs, *Production and Stage Management at the Blackfriars Theatre* (1933).

108. **Knutson, Roslyn L.** *The Repertory of Shakespeare's Company, 1594–1613.* Fayetteville: Univ. of Arkansas Press, 1991.

Knutson begins with an overview of repertory procedures in the commercial theatre and of their related financial operations. She then investigates what is known of these activities by the Lord Chamberlain's Men (1594–1603) and of their subsequent similar operations as the King's Men (1603–1613). Her concluding section identifies the specific role of the works of Shakespeare within these basic administrative and financial procedures of a commercial repertory theater. The author establishes the administrative context which sustains most theatres, including Shakespeare's, and which powerfully affects most artistic choices.

109. **McGuire, Philip C.** *Speechless Dialect: Shakespeare's Open Silences.* Berkeley: Univ. of California Press, 1985.

McGuire discusses the theatrical effect of key characters' failure to speak at climaxes of representative plays: Viola, Sebastian, Antonio, and Aguecheek in *Twelfth Night*; Hippolyta in *Dream*; Barnadine and Isabella in *Measure*; Edgar in the Quarto *Lear*; Antonio and Ariel in *Tempest*. The range of "open" meanings latent in such gaps is illustrated from the contrasting, skeptical interpretations in recent productions, which tend to favor negative readings (such as assigning Isabella a silent rejection of the Duke's marriage proposal at the end of *Measure*). This flexibility explains Shakespeare's adaptability to evolving cultural contexts. The interpretations offer modern insights into Shakespeare's theatrical practices and his openness to different readings. The more traditional, positive interpretations of such silences as Isabella's appear in A. Thaler, *Shakespeare's Silences.* Cambridge: Harvard Univ. Press, 1929.

110. **Montrose, Louis.** *The Purpose of Playing: Shakespeare and the Cultural Politics of the Elizabethan Theatre.* Chicago: Univ. of Chicago Press, 1996.

Part 1 of this study in New Historicism uses Shakespeare's tragedies and histories to display "the politics of representation" (xi) in Elizabethan culture and society in terms of drama's relation to authority in metropolitan London, in a period of religious, economic, and social change. Part 2 of Montrose's book uses modern concepts of gender and family more locally as a means of explicating relationships in a comedy, *Dream*. In his main arguments, Montrose follows Weimann (no. 123) in thinking that theatre undermines authority in part by its demonstration of the universality of artifice. This study offers an explanation for the sustained opposition to theatre performances in the city of London by its Corporation, justifying the scrutiny of scripts for subsversive implications, when submitted for approval to the Master of the Revels. See also the broader treatment of the implications of Elizabethan performances in Stephen Greenblatt, *Shakespearean Negotiations* (1988). A similarly influential argument has been applied to the political implications of Stuart drama in Stephen Orgel, *The Illusions of Power* (1975). These views of the effect on Shakespearean performances of the authority of the royal courts are modified in Kernan (no. 104).

111. **Muir, Kenneth, Jay Halio, and D. J. Palmer, eds.** *Shakespeare, Man of the Theater.* Newark: Univ. of Delaware Press, 1983.

This volume records the proceedings of the Second Congress of the International Shakespeare Association in 1981, with essays by, among others, Stephen Orgel on Shakespeare's concepts of theaters and audiences; Emrys Jones on the use of night sequences; Anne Barton on Shakespeare's relation to Jonson; Philip Edwards on Shakespeare and Kyd; Bernard Beckerman on historic and iconic time; Jeanne Roberts on eighteenth-century actresses in Shakespearean comedy; Adele Seefe on Charles Kean's *Lear*; and Robert Weimann on theatre relations to authority. The anthology provides a cross-section of scholarly concerns about Shakespearean production.

111a. **Stephen Orgel.** *Impersonations: the Performance of Gender in Shakespeare's England.* Cambridge: Cambridge Univ. Press, 1996.

Orgel surveys recent research about gender in Elizabethan society, not only in terms of male and female roles on- and off-stage, but also in connection with the implications of the transvestism involved in the use of boy actors on the Elizabethan stage, particularly as seen in such examples as Shakespeare's Viola and Rosalind. Following New Historicist procedures, Orgel is concerned to interpret Shakespeare's plays in the light of Elizabethan social practices generally, as redefined by current gender theory, for which he finds precedents in P. Stallybrass, "Transvestism and the 'Body Beneath': Speculating on the Boy Actor." In S. Zimmerman, ed. *Erotic Politics: Desire on the Renaissance Stage*, 64–83 (1992). See also

L. Levine, *Men in Women's Clothing: Antitheatricality and Effeminization 1579–1642* (1994). For an earlier, more comprehensive performance study of Shakespeare's use of boy actors, see no. 92.

112. **Richman, David.** *Laughter, Pain, and Wonder: Shakespeare's Comedies and the Audience in the Theater.* Newark: Univ. of Delaware Press, 1990.

Richman attempts to identify audience reactions both to the original performances of the comedies and to modern ones, contrasting them with reader responses by close reference to specific recent productions. He stresses the scripts' calculated emotional progression. This book is one of the few to attempt a detailed account of the plays in terms of their likely emotional effects on live audiences. It tends to apply modern moral and social values which make the comedies' resolutions seem incomplete and less satisfying.

113. **Righter, Anne [Barton].** *Shakespeare and the Idea of the Play.* London: Chatto and Windus, 1962.

This book urges use of the play as a subject of discussion in its own text. Part One covers the audience as actor in mysteries and moralities. Righter explores the evolution from classical comedy and hybrids, in which the play's artificiality is indirectly noted by increasing references to the audience, leading to later full equation of the outside World and the Stage, achieved through theatrical experiments involving new audience attitudes. Part Two looks at play imagery in early Shakespeare; his Player Kings and Lords of Misrule; the power of a play's credibility for those on stage, as in *Hamlet*; the devaluation of staging in *Macbeth*; and the final full equation of stage, dreams, and reality in the last plays. While recognizing the dramatist's self-consciousness in his art, the book forces the extent of Shakespeare's self-allusions in his scripts.

114. **Ringler, William A.** "The Number of Actors in Shakespeare's Early Plays." In no. 154: 110–36.

Ringler examines the casting practices of the Lord Chamberlain's company in Shakespeare's first eighteen plays through *Henry V* and *Caesar*. He considers the minimum numbers for their performance, with limited doubling resulting from unbroken performance between scenes. The essay argues that this flow would not permit costume changes between successive scenes, and that scenes with large casts alternate with ones with smaller numbers, so major groups can shift costumes. There are doubling tables for *Caesar, Love's Labour's,* and *Dream,* showing that casts of sixteen are required, including two to four boys. Ringler finds this number suits later plays, except for *Henry VIII,* while one early play, *Two Gentlemen,* requires a cast of only ten. Against most modern practice, he argues that in *Dream,* by Elizabethan precedents of time provided for costume changes in doubling, Titania should not double as Hippolyta, but that the fairies may double as workmen. The topic of doubling is developed in R. Fotheringham, "The Doubling of Roles on the Jacobean Stage," *Theatre Research International* 10 (1985): 18–32.

115. **Shirley, Frances Ann.** *Shakespeare's Use of Off-Stage Sounds.* Lincoln: Univ. of Nebraska Press, 1963.

Shirley examines the use and production of offstage sounds in Shakespeare's plays, particularly *Caesar, Hamlet,* and *Macbeth.* An appendix lists all the sounds needed in performing Shakespeare.

116. **Skura, Meredith A.** *Shakespeare the Actor and the Purposes of Playing.* Chicago: Univ. of Chicago Press, 1993.

Skura attempts to reconstruct "the mental climate in which Shakespeare's plays were written, particularly those aspects affecting and affected by his experience as an actor" (ix). While noting political and economic constraints, Skura stresses psycholanalytic considerations: the unconscious; "overdetermined" theater; private versus public issues; role-playing; and the psychology of performance criticism. She considers actors' feelings of professional ambivalence in playing Clowns and Epilogues. She treats *Richard III* as autobiography; considers the player king as mere beggar in great houses; reviews theory, as in Hamlet's concept of drama as mirror to audiences; treats the performer as variously flatterer, pet, and victim. She reviews Shakespeare's references to acting, and ends with the effect of the Globe circle on audience self-awareness.

117. **Slater, Ann Pasternak.** *Shakespeare the Director.* Brighton, U.K.: Harvester; and Totowa N. J.: Barnes and Noble, 1982.

Slater examines the detailed directorial instructions in Shakespeare's text, covering acting style; position on the stage; taking by the hand, kneeling, kissing, and embracing; weeping; silence and pauses; costumes and disguises; properties. These specifications are related to sources, subplots, and exact meanings. The detailed analyses show how specific situations in scripts are designed to work on the stage. The broader conclusion is that Elizabethan stage practice, never consistently formal, progressed towards greater realism without losing symbolic, allegorical, or moralistic overtones. An index covers types of stage business, and there is a bibliography.

118. **Smith, Warren D.** *Shakespeare's Playhouse Practice: A Handbook.* Hanover, N.H.: Univ. Press of New England, 1975.

In this short book, Smith surveys the stage practices involved in producing an Elizabethan play, and includes well-established procedures for stage entries; for physical business identifiable during dialogues; for blocking in relation to such stage features as the down-stage pillars; for the character and use of stage properties; for the handling of soliloquies, asides, and apostrophes; for the use of the upper stage; for the role of the prompter; and for the sign-posting and handling of exits. He makes use of evidence included in the scripts' spoken language and in their printed stage directions, derived chiefly from Shakespearean texts. He demonstrates that, despite the absence of elaborate stage directions typical of modern play texts, Shakespeare characteristically embeds in his scripts clear signals to his actors about their physical action through incidental clues or formal cues in what he makes them say. Often these cues are so frequent as to be consistent conventions, such as the use of a rhyming couplet before exits and scene closures. Smith argues that some of the clues ensure actors' appropriate behavior and that others are intended to alert audiences to what is happening. His observations about how scripts are keyed to performance are helpful to directors and actors, as well as to students and critics.

119. **Sprague, Arthur Colby.** *Shakespeare and the Audience: A Study in the Technique of Exposition.* Cambridge: Harvard Univ. Press, 1935.

Sprague compares the techniques of exposition in novels and plays, covering establishment of time and place (such as scenery in *Lear*, or night settings in other plays). Next he covers use of conventions: soliloquies, asides, whispers, and letters. He notes that beginnings and endings require identifications of characters, and that plots require audience preparation as well as use of surprise and recapitulation by initiators such as Friar Laurence. He finds that characters comment chorically on each other and the action, and that villains and heroes serve as mutual foils, sometimes misrepresenting each others' motives instructively. The book addresses audience concerns systematically.

120. **Stopes, Charlotte C.** *Burbage and Shakespeare's Stage.* London: Alexander Moring, 1913.

This biography of the Burbage family stresses the business activities of James and Richard Burbage, as shown in contemporary references. It is fully annotated ("Authorities": 145–263), including citations from numerous lawsuits and pleas. This text facilitates study of the Burbages despite its early date, providing essential circumstantial background for Shakespeare studies from records about the Theatre, the Globe Theatre, and the Blackfriars Theatre, though the book makes little literary application of its data.

121. **Styan, John L.** "In Search of the Real Shakespeare; or Shakespeare's Shows and Shadows." In no. 78.

This essay is a pendant to no. 25, illustrating how that study's concerns with Shakespearean staging might be investigated by use of such a resource as Sam Wanamaker's reconstruction of the first Globe Theatre. Styan considers live audience's reactions to such non-realistic effects as use of boy actors for women's roles, to the actors' intimate physical closeness to the audience in soliloquies and asides, to implausible blocking (e.g., of overhearings), to abrupt shifts of characterization, and to variable awareness in acknowledging stage artifice. Styan argues that by such effects a restored

Elizabethan theatre must diminish the reader's dominance in Shakespeare studies. See nos. 78, 293.

122. **Venezky, Alice S.** *Pageantry on the Shakespearean Stage.* New York: Twayne, 1951.

This book shows the influence of processions, pageants, and progresses on Elizabethan drama, particularly Shakespeare's. It covers entries and triumphs on stage and as described, for example, in *Richard II, Richard III,* and *Henry V,* among others noted here. It considers royal receptions (orations, songs, entertainments, gifts) in texts including, among others, *Measure* and *Richard III.* It notes pageants, progresses, plays, dumb-shows, allegories, tableaux, provincial tours, country settings, and amateur performances in such plays as *Dream, Love's Labour's,* and *Macbeth.* It links the formulas of Petrarch's *Trionfi* (which rehearse the triumphs of Love, Death, Time) to imagery in, among other plays, *Henry VI,* the pastoral comedies, and *Tempest.* The appendix provides a bibliography and a chronology of "Royal Celebrations, 1298–1623." The book reconsiders the significance of the ritual and processional elements which occur in most of Shakespeare's plays. The topic reappears in papers at the International Shakespeare Association in 1981, published in *Pageantry in the Shakespearean Theater,* ed. D. Bergeron (1985).

123. **Weimann, Robert.** *Shakespeare and the Popular Tradition in the Theater: Studies in the Social Dimension of Dramatic Form and Function.* Baltimore: Johns Hopkins Univ. Press, 1978.

First published in German in 1967, this study of pre-Shakespearean forms of popular performance covers the fool; folkplays; the mystery cycles, moralities, and interludes; the earlier Elizabethan drama with its popularized humanism; and the Shakespearean theater. These topics are related to Shakespearean scripts with explicit allusions to earlier popular modes and practices, confirming these as a dominant influence. Weimann distinguishes between the use of upper stages for authority figures and lower stages nearer the audience for clowns and ordinary roles. He argues that his definitions of the unlocalized *platea* and the specific *locus* in earlier drama herald the distinction between the main stage and the inner and upper playing spaces in Elizabethan theaters. With his dense and exact references, Weimann's Marxist stance provides a populist balance to academic stress on humanist elements in Shakespeare's drama.

124. **Wiles, David.** *Shakespeare's Clowns: Actor and Text in the Elizabethan Playhouse.* Cambridge: Cambridge Univ. Press, 1987.

Wiles traces the Elizabethan clown's early dominance in Shakespeare to the assertiveness of the medieval Vice in *Mankind,* which is not naturalistic but invites aesthetic and moral judgment. He shows Tarlton as the first clown, followed by Will Kempe, with his jigs. He finds that the Clown had a free hand in post-performance entertainment. Wiles sees the Clown as a conventional, not a psychological character, as is proved by Kempe's roles: Launce, Costard, Bottom, and Dogberry. Yet he shows how such a character promotes changes in the various texts of *Romeo*. Wiles contrasts Kempe's earlier roles with that of Falstaff, also Kempe's. Wiles argues that Kempe validated Falstaff's assertion that "I shall be sent for soon" at the end of *2 Henry IV* (5.5.89), when Kempe's jig followed the show. Wiles thinks that Falstaff's failure to reappear in *Henry V* results from Kempe's dismissal. He ends with Armin, a "natural" Fool because of his dwarfish, doglike physique (natural in the role of Thersites). An appendix discusses Armin's "motley." The last chapter is on "Theory," but the book's revolutionary idea is that Kempe's influence on the audience was conclusive: "the jig allows the audience to deconstruct the finale of the play" (56), as also seen in Clowns' appearances at climaxes (Cleopatra's death or Ophelia's burial). See no. 96.

See also nos. 2, 12, 13, 15, 16, 17, 19, 20, 25, 26, 33, 34, 35, 37, 39, 42, 45, 47, 50, 52, 53, 54, 55, 56, 59, 61, 63, 68, 70, 82, 85, 139, 140, 151, 292, 293.

III. SHAKESPEAREAN STAGE HISTORY: 1616–1998

A. OVERVIEWS 1616–1998

125. Arnott, James Fullerton, and John William Robinson. *English Theatrical Literature 1559–1900; A Bibliography incorporating Robert Lowe's "A Bibliographical Account of English Theatrical Literature" (published in 1888).* London: Library of the Society for Theatre Research, 1970.

This reference work has review sections under the headings of Bibliography, Government Regulation, Morality, Arts of the Theatre, General History, London Theatre, Theatre Out of London, Opera, Irregular and Amateur Theatre, Theory and Criticism, and Periodicals. Indexes cover authors, short titles, and places of publication. Bibliographical entries include summaries. Items bear on the history of Shakespearean performance. Elaborately cross-referenced, this book assists identification of original documents and secondary sources up to 1900.

126. Bate, Jonathan, and Russell Jackson, eds. *Shakespeare: An Illustrated History.* Oxford: Oxford Univ. Press, 1996.

This anthology has 112 illustrations. It includes essays about Shakespeare production by Reginald A. Foakes on Elizabethan stages; Martin Wiggins on the King's Men; Peter Holland on Garrick's era; Jonathan Bate on the Romantic stage; Russell Jackson on actor-managers; Inga-Stina Ewbank on Shakespeare's influence on European drama; Anthony Davis on the Old Vic; Peter Thomson on government support; Robert Smallwood on directors; Judi Dench on acting; and Russell Jackson on recent trends.

There is a current bibliography. The book provides a summary of current knowledge and views about the history of Shakespearean performance.

127. **Berry, Ralph.** *Shakespeare in Performance: Casting and Metamorphosis.* London: Macmillan, 1993.

Berry begins with the interpretational implications of casting: the doubling and tripling of actors required by such a text as *Hamlet*, in which Marcellus may reappear as Fortinbras; the effects of casting Hamlet as a contemporary rebel or as a traditional Renaissance prince; the treatment of extras in crowd scenes as sympathetic Chorus or alien Mobs in *Caesar* and *Coriolanus*; the casting of Ariel as male or female; the casting of the Duchess of York in *Richard II* as a comic role. He reviews implications of stage directions and speech prefixes as keys to characterization in the Folio, Quartos, and regularized modern editions. The text is discursive but raises exact points about the dramatist's concept of his characters.

128. **Conolly, Leonard W., and J. P. Wearing, eds.** *English Drama and Theatre, 1800–1900: A Guide to Information Sources.* Detroit: Gale Research Co., 1978.

This comprehensive bibliography of research (including dissertations) includes numerous items about 19th-century Shakespearean performance, as well as theatre histories, critiques, and biographies of actors, managers, designers, and critics. It remains useful, but can be supplemented by *Shakespeare: A Bibliographical Guide,* ed. S. Wells, 52–68. (1973, revised, 1990). This section covers "Shakespeare in Performance, 1660 to the Present," with a substantial bibliography, prepared by M. Jamieson.

129. **Dawson, Anthony B.** *Watching Shakespeare: A Playgoers' Guide.* New York: St. Martin's, 1988.

Dawson explores how modern productions of eighteen major Shakespeare plays use current professional options: traditional proscenium format with the scenery and verisimilitude of Irving and Tree compared to open-stage and Brechtian styles; high rhetoric versus Method inwardness as in the Othellos of Olivier versus Hopkins; Brook's circus *Dream* contrasted with the Mendelssohnian fairy tradition of Reinhardt; problems in shrinking *Lear*'s cosmic scale to confined stages; various periodizations of *Hamlet*. These informal accounts illustrate current approaches to staging Shakespeare.

130. **Dobbs, Brian.** *Drury Lane: Three Centuries of the Theatre Royal 1663–1971.* London: Cassell, 1972.

This overview discusses such issues as the effect of the coming of actresses to the English stage at the Restoration, and other theatrical and administrative matters in one of the major London theatres. It often alludes to Shakespeare in noting such artistic concerns as the effect of Betterton's stage manner and the impact of Macklin's spectacular Shylock in 1741, but it does not cover individual productions in detail, as does the more informal account in W. J. Macqueen Pope, *Theatre Royal, Drury Lane* (no date).

131. **Dunn, Esther Cloudman.** *Shakespeare in America.* New York: Macmillan, 1939.

Dunn's Chapter II covers the first 100 years; III, the pre-revolutionary 18th century; IV, London's impact on Colonial culture; VI and VII, Shakespeare in the Revolution; IX, the first fifty years of the U.S.A.; X, the Ohio and Mississippi Valleys; XI, the Gold Rush. The other chapters treat magazines, education, thought, and scholarship rather than performance. The book provides an overview, not detailed information about single productions.

132. **Goldman, Michael.** *Shakespeare and the Energies of Drama.* Princeton: Princeton Univ. Press, 1972.

Goldman applies current ideas about subjectivity to Shakespearean characters' and actors' relations to audiences, seen as strained in the role of Henry V. His discussions of challenges to actors include how to maintain the kinetic energy of Romeo and Juliet; how to communicate the abundance and multiplicity of Falstaff as well as his vulnerability and pathos; how to achieve audience involvement with Hamlet's dilemma; and how to register the experience of Lear's extreme of misery. In addition to insights into individual roles, this book establishes the actor-audience relationship as the unique nexus of drama for modern students of the text, as well as of staging. The values are mostly modern, but Goldman's analysis illuminates the original dramatist's probable character and concerns. See also M. Goldman, *Acting and Action in Shakespearean Tragedy* (1985).

133. **Grebanier, Bernard.** *Then Came Each Actor.* New York: David McKay, 1975.

This overview of Shakespearean production from Elizabethan times to the 20th century provides highlights for each period, with a largely biographical approach focussed on the principal professional personalities, but raising issues of staging and interpretation, with a chapter on silent films, and a selective account of more recent work, focussed on Gielgud and Olivier. The style is informal, but Grebanier uses substantial sources and identifies basic concerns, such as the emphasis on racial issues in recent productions of *Othello*.

134. **Halstead, William P.** *Shakespeare as Spoken: A Collation of 5,000 Acting Editions and Promptbooks of Shakespeare.* 12 Vols. Ann Arbor: Univ. Microfilms International, for the American Theater Association, 1977–80.

This vast work covers thirty-seven plays under individual titles, three or four to each volume, in "a collation of all acting editions and promptbooks in English through 1975 of professional productions held in public collections" (I.xii). It proceeds only by changes affecting a full verse line, so most local word and phrase adaptations are not considered, and they are recorded only when they alter the sense. It refers only to printed scripts, mostly those using more than 70% of Shakespeare's text, and prepared by any actor, director, manager, or publisher. Each left-hand page prints the relevant lines from the Globe *Works of William Shakespeare*, ed. G. Clark and W. A. Wright (1867). There are extensive source bibliographies for each play. The compression of the references and the extensive abbreviations make this text hard to follow, but it contains much information about successive and substantial textual modifications of Shakespeare for performance over the centuries.

135. **Homan, Sidney, ed.** *Shakespeare's "More Than Words Can Witness": Essays on Visual and Nonverbal Enactment in the Plays.* Lewisburg, Pa: Bucknell Univ. Press, 1980.

The book collects twelve essays on how visual staging of Shakespeare affects meaning, including Maurice Charney on the effects of props and costumes; Alfred Harbage on "Choral Juxtaposition"; Robert Hapgood on "Choreography and Timing"; Bernard Beckerman on "Expectations of Elizabethan and Modern 'Playgoing'"; Barbara Hodgdon on "Shakespeare's Directorial Eye," for irony (see no. 107); Terence Hawkes on the actors' physiological contribution to scripts; accounts of visual patternings on stage by Alan Dessen; discussion of wordlessness by Tommy Ruth Waldo; and a final essay by the editor on filmic imagery. The book displays the meanings added to the script by visual effects of performance. See also S. Homan, *Shakespeare's Theatre of Presence: Language, Spectacle and Audience* (1986).

136. **Kelly, F. M.** *Shakespeare Costume for Stage and Screen.* London: Adam and Charles Black, 1938. Revised by Alan Mansfield, 1970. Repr., corrected, 1973.

Kelly explains and illustrates scripts' terms for costume as these terms were used in references made by historical texts from 1560 to 1620. He describes the clothing worn by men, women, the military, and many other wearers of distinctive costume, as they relate to different theatrical genres. He covers costume-making methods and sources for material, and he provides a bibliography, which Mansfield has updated. Mansfield includes new illustrations, and he has taken into account new museum collections, and expanded coverage of male and female dress, of foreign costumes, and of armor. The book provides advice for the period costuming of modern productions.

137. **Marshall, Norman.** *The Producer and the Play.* London: MacDonald, 1958. Revised, 1962.

Marshall displays the dominant role of the modern producer/director in a full range of 20th-century theatre productions, in which Shakespeare figures prominently, from the extravagant realism of Beerbohm Tree's productions, through the revision of their standards in the light of Poel's Elizabethan theatrical historicism and the related innovations of Granville-Barker and Gordon Craig, down to the provocative experimentalism of Guthrie and Brook. While Shakespeare proves a touchstone for evolving tastes throughout the book, three central chapters specifically review productions of his plays: in the period from the 17th century to Granville-Barker; during the subsequent break with this tradition; and in the period since 1940. The text is richly illustrated, mostly showing Shakespearean productions, and it reflects the author's direct observations of most modern major productions discussed. Significant developments up to 1962 receive informed comment, and references to current celebrities like Zeffirelli and Hall ensure that the text remains relevant to recent work in the theatre. This perceptive guide comprehensively explicates the modern western theatre tradition.

138. **McGuire, Philip C., and David Samuelson, eds.** *Shakespeare: The Theatrical Dimension.* AMS Studies in the Renaissance, Vol. 3. New York: AMS Press, 1979.

This anthology of essays stresses modern interpretations of Shakespeare offered in recent performances. Miriam Gilbert discusses role-playing in the exchange of their roles as Richard II and Bolingbroke by Richard Pasco and Ian Richardson during the run of John Barton's *Richard II* (1973), and Philip McGuire discusses textual indications for stage choreography, also in *Richard II*. Stephen Booth considers doubling in the plays. Douglas Sprigg notes how the seduction of Cressida can be staged. Bernard Beckerman shows how the vast themes of *Antony* are reduced to chamber-music scale. There are also essays by Marvin Rosenberg (on poetry), John Styan (on character), John Russell Brown (on *Twelfth Night*), and Michael Goldman (on *Hamlet*).

139. **Merchant, W. Moelwyn,** *Shakespeare and the Artist.* London: Oxford Univ. Press, 1959.

This text examines numerous illustrations to show how scholars can apply examples from the Visual Arts to illuminate the meaning of specific scripts and the intent of local allusions to these Arts in plays, including the use or mention of music, stage sets, and lighting. Part 1 covers the Elizabethan theatre and the Visual Arts, ranging down to the 20th century. Part 2 discusses specific examples of productions' use of the Visual Arts, focusing on the use of the Arts in particular productions of *Timon, Coriolanus, Lear, Henry VIII, Winter's Tale,* and *Measure.*

140. **Salgado, Gamini.** *Eyewitnesses of Shakespeare: First Hand Accounts of Performances 1590–1890.* London: Chatto & Windus for Sussex Univ. Press, 1975.

This anthology provides excerpts from classic performance commentaries on Shakespeare from the start of his career. It begins in Part I with exhaustive 16th- and 17th-century references. The much more selective commentaries quoted in Part II for the period 1700–1890 are arranged under relevant play titles, often with illustrations. Some sources are unfamiliar: Goldsmith's account of a touring production of *Romeo* for which the costumes were one coat, a piece of crepe, and some bed-sheets; or Lewis Carroll's *Diaries'* praise of Kean's 1855 production of "the great play *Henry VIII*, the greatest theatrical treat I ever had or ever expect to have" (352). There are indexes of contributors and performers. A more local study of early audiences is R. Levin, "Women in the Renaissance Theatre Audience," *Shakespeare Quarterly* 40 (1989): 165–74.

141. **Schmidgall, Gary.** *Shakespeare and Opera.* Oxford: Oxford Univ. Press, 1990.

Despite its title and a concluding critique of some major operas derived from Shakespeare, this book does not fully survey the operatic versions of Shakespeare, but argues for the superior relevance of operatic aesthetics to the understanding of Shakespearean performance in comparison with modern realistic conventions in staging plays. There are correlations of Shakespearean scripts and operatic analogues, particularly by Verdi, but the book argues for the non-realistic nature of Shakespearean staging and its affinities for musical interpretation by its heightened rhetoric and melodramatic situations, the stress on the sound of language, the concern for the exact vocal talents of performers, and the superiority of artistic skill to physical appearances. The comparisons achieve striking aperçus, such as Shakespeare's exact calculation of the vocal limits of boy actors in women's roles, but the book is primarily discursive, not systematic or theoretical.

142. *Shakespearean Criticism: Excerpts from the Criticism of William Shakespeare's Plays and Poetry, from the First Published Appraisals to Current Evaluations.* Detroit: Gale Research, 1984–.

Some of the later volumes in this series exhaustively survey and excerpt important accounts of the performance history of Shakespeare's plays, several of which are collected for each volume in random groups, in quantities determined by the popularity of the chosen titles. There are critical bibliographies of publications about each script's performance history. These anthologies are very helpful starting points for study of any included script's performance history. The series is in progress.

143. **Shattuck, Charles H.** "'Shakespeare's Plays in Performance from 1660 to the Present." Appendix A in *Riverside Shakespeare*, no. 2, 1905–31.

Shattuck's extensive essay covers the history of Shakespeare production in English from the Restoration reopening of the theatres, providing an overview of factors in the evolution of Shakespeare performance. It includes sections on American and on cinematic productions. While it cannot provide full details about any phase of its coverage, the essay highlights significant individuals, issues, and achievements in Shakespearean staging. See also the new Appendix B in the 1997 edition: W. T. Liston, "Shakespeare's Plays in Performance from 1970," pp. 1932–1950. Liston reviews significant recent productions in England, the U.S.A., Canada, and elsewhere since Shattuck's essay was written, with notes on film and television and the restored Globe Theatre in Southwark. He also includes a bibliography for the later period.

144. **Shattuck, Charles H.** *Shakespeare on the American Stage: From the Hallams to Edwin Booth;* and *From Booth and Barrett to Sothern and Marlowe.* 2 vols. Washington: Folger Shakespeare Library, 1976 and 1987.

In Volume 1 of this richly illustrated book, Shattuck surveys the first two centuries in the history of American Shakespeare production from 1752, with the Hallams, down to the times of Edwin Booth. He centers later essays around such major theatrical figures as William Charles Macready, Edwin Forrest, James Hackett, Charlotte Cushman, William Evans Burton, George Frederick Cooke, Anne Brunton Marry, E. L. Davenport, John McCullough, and Junius Brutus Booth. Volume 2 extends this survey to cover the fifty years ending after the conclusion of World War I with the founding of Equity in 1919. The second volume concentrates on the partnership and tours of Booth and Barrett; Daly's productions of the comedies; the feminizing effect of Victorian actresses such as Langtree, Modjeska, and Bernhardt; and the end of the tradition in Mansfield, Mantell, Sothern, and Marlowe. Shattuck stresses the anti-Shakespearean effect of the Syndicate's nationwide control of bookings from 1896 onwards, and his Epilogue discusses the Shakespeare Tercentenary. Shattuck considers the latest periods of Shakespeare production too complex to cover.

145. **Shattuck, Charles H.** *The Shakespeare Promptbooks: a Descriptive Catalogue.* Urbana: Univ. of Illinois Press, 1965.

Shattuck lists known prompt books up to 1961, with some later additions, play by play in alphabetical order. He gives the actor, director, prompter, or stage manager associated with each promptbook; then the city, theatre or country of its use, and the date; next he cites its location at present, with its call number; finally he provides a physical description of each script, with an account of its contents and of the stage directions included. This record offers data about many significant productions but only a few of the total of historical performances.

146. **Speaight, Robert.** *Shakespeare on the Stage: An Illustrated History of Shakespearian Performance.* London: Collins, 1973.

This overview for "the general playgoer" covers the period 1574–1965, mostly accepting A. C. Sprague's emphases (nos. 147, 148) for earlier periods and J. C. Trewin's theatrical perspective (nos. 220, 222, 223) for the 20th century. The 16th and 17th centuries are briefly treated, a third of the book covers the 18th and 19th centuries, and fully half reviews the 20th century. Theatrical organization and staging are summarized, with stress on the personalities of actors (such as "Eminent Tragedians," and Irving's work at the Lyceum Theatre) and directors (such as Beerbohm Tree, Lilian Baylis, and Tyrone Guthrie). The text notes unfamiliar items like the 1821 productions of *Othello* and *Richard III* in New York by black actors led by James Hewlett; early difficulties with Shakespeare on French stages; tensions between Gordon Craig and Stanislavsky in producing *Hamlet*; productions in non-English-speaking countries (France, Italy, Russia, and Germany, noting Max Reinhardt). American performances listed include those of the Barrymores and Margaret Webster. Distinctive illustrations cover actors (such as the Cushman sisters as Romeo and Juliet), costumes, and scenic designs (Orson Welles' "voodoo" *Macbeth*). The author debates such questions as whether Shylock should be treated as tragic. There is no coverage of late 20th century film or television. Despite selectivity, the text is an excellent introduction to theatre history.

147. **Sprague, Arthur Colby.** *Shakespeare and the Actors: The Stage Business in his Plays (1660–1905).* Cambridge, Mass.: Harvard Univ. Press, 1945. Repr., New York: Russell and Russell, 1963.

Chapters cover, play by play, comedies (with romances); histories; *Hamlet*; *Othello*; *Macbeth*; other tragedies. The procedure is the accumulation of historical stage business play by play. For example, Viola has beeen variously shown as either frightened or confident in her fight with Aguecheek; and, as Queen Katherine, Mrs. Siddons' aggressiveness towards Cardinal Wolsey in *Henry VIII* provided a classic interpretative point accepted ever since. The selected details highlight issues still relevant in many cases, but the data are not as comprehensive as M. Rosenberg's series of single-play studies of the major tragedies, beginning with *The Masks of Othello* (1961), for which Sprague's work provided a precedent. Fuller historical detail does appear in A. C. Sprague, *Shakespearean Players and Performances* (1953).

148. **Sprague, Arthur Colby.** *Shakespeare's Histories: Plays for the Stage.* London: Society for Theatre Research, 1966.

This overview of productions of Shakespeare's history plays, from his time to the mid–20th century, reviews each play in terms of the performance options dictated by the characteristic cultural and stage values of each period, as reflected in original sources such as prompt books and contemporary reviews, as well as the author's own observations of modern productions. Ironically, the occasion of the book, Shakespeare's fourth centenary, led to such productions as the English history cycle of John Barton and Peter Hall (Royal Shakespeare Company, 1964) with revolutionary treatment of the histories unanticipated in this study.

149. **Stamm, Rudolf.** *Shakespeare's Word Scenery with Some Remarks on Stage History and the Interpretation of His Plays.* Zurich and St. Gallen: Polygraphischer Verlag, 1954.

Assuming a play is completed only in performance, this text surveys and evaluates performance methodology, using *Macbeth* to contrast Elizabethan verbal versions to modern stage literalism in conditioning audiences about such effects as darkness and other aspects of sets and setting. It uses *As You Like It, Merchant of Venice*, and the *Henry V* Chorus to explain means of establishing a location. The author censures the counterproductive effect of elaborate and realistic scenery, lighting, and sound effects in making the spoken script inaudible or redundant. The role of music is stressed. The arguments are salutary and remain current.

150. **Thompson, Marvin and Ruth, eds.** *Shakespeare and the Sense of Performance: Essays in the Tradition of Performance Criticism in Honor of Bernard Beckerman.* Newark: Univ. of Delaware Press, 1989.

This book illustrates Beckerman's performance criticism through a bibliography of his work and through essays sharing his approach by leaders in the field. After an overview of modern performance critics by the editors, Ralph Berry writes of Hamlet's relation to the audience; Inga-Stina Ewbank and John Russell Brown consider stage language; Alan Dessen and John Styan write of the use and meaning of space on the Elizabethan stage; Homer Swander and Michael Goldman compare Shakespeare's staging with that of Beckett and that of Marlowe; Marvin Rosenberg and Albert Braunmuller consider implicit and editorial stage directions; Glynne Wickham and Hugh Richmond review modern production procedures in the light of Shakespearean contexts; detailed aspects of staging are discussed by Maurice Charney (asides and soliloquies), Reginald Foakes (stage imagery), Andrew Gurr (thrones), Derek Peat (the Lords' Room). Thomas Clayton ends with a skeptical review of flamboyant effects in modern productions, arguing for the primacy of the script's authentic language on the audience over interpolated "production values."

151. **Watkins, Ronald.** *On Producing Shakespeare.* London: Michael Joseph, 1950. Repr., New York: Benjamin Bloom, 1964.

This encyclopedic survey of Shakespearean theatre practices covers the use of theatre space (following J. Cranford Adams), acting procedures (following T. W. Baldwin on speech, mime, characterization, boy actors); functions of poetry (atmosphere, character). It concludes by applying them to a production of *Macbeth*. The book is somewhat dated in its research data, but covers a range of stage interpretations of classic Shakespearean passages in Elizabethan terms.

152. **Winter, William.** *Shakespeare on the Stage.* New York: Moffat, Yard, 1911 (First Series); 1915 (Second Series); 1916 (Third Series).

These three volumes provide surveys of factors and of principal actors in the history of performance of a selection of the plays: *Richard III, Merchant, Hamlet, Othello, Macbeth, Henry VIII* (First Series); *Twelfth Night, Romeo, Lear, Shrew, Caesar* (Second Series); *Cymbeline, Love's Labour's, Dream, Henry IV, Merry Wives, Antony, John* (Third Series). Winter covers early and late performances, British and American ones in historical sequence, tending to summaries and lists, but including less obvious data, such as Augustin Daly's two New York productions of *Love's Labour's* in 1858 and 1891 (III.190–95). There are Indexes of Actors and Managers, Characters, and Titles, but the work is selective, discursive, and personal.

153. **Worthen, W. B.** *Shakespeare and the Authority of Performance.* Cambridge: Cambridge Univ. Press, 1997.

Worthen surveys current debate about the relationship between the various edited texts of Shakespeare and the range in performance of them, with the intention of resolving the relationship between the author "Shakespeare" and the range of modern interpretations offered on stage as alternatives to critical readings of him. Worthen outlines the various strategies and claims made by modern directors, actors, and scholars, paying particlar attention to the work of directors such as Brook, Miller, and Sellars, and of actors such as Stewart, Callow, Sher, Pennington, and Cox. He pays particular attention to *Merchant* as a key test of modern attitudes. In conclusion, Worthen attempts to resolve the challenges to the authority of performance raised by H. Berger, *Imaginary Auditions: Shakespeare on Stage and Page* (1989), and the historical relativism registered in G. Taylor, *Reinventing Shakespeare: A Cultural History from the Restoration to the Present* (1991). See also W. B. Worthen. "The Deeper Meanings and Theatrical Technique: the Rhetoric of Performance Criticism." *Shakespeare Quarterly* 44: 441–55.

See also nos. 1, 2, 6, 7, 10, 12, 22, 26, 97.

B. Early Performances: 1616–1642

154. Bentley, Gerald E., ed. *The Seventeenth-Century Stage: A Collection of Critical Essays.* Chicago: Univ. of Chicago Press, 1968.

Part I contains extracts about Renaissance drama by Dekker, Heywood, Jonson, and Brome. Part II covers Actors and Acting, with essays by John Russell Brown, Muriel Bradbrook, Michael Jamieson, Marvin Rosenberg, and William Ringler (see no. 114). Part III, on Theatres and Production, includes F. P. Wilson on the scrivener Ralph Crane; Louis B. Wright on Duels; Richard Hosley on the Discovery Space; William Armstrong on the Elizabethan Audiences of Private Theatres; and J. W. Saunders on Staging at the Globe 1599–1613. The focus is on Elizabethan and Jacobean material.

155. Edwards, Philip, Gerald Eades Bentley, Kathleen McLuskie, and Lois Potter. *The Revels History of Drama in English, Volume IV, 1613–60.* London: Methuen, 1981.

The first part of this survey, "Society and the Theatre," by

Philip Edwards, includes essays on the court, royalty, the nobility, managers, dramatists and their economics, audiences, play performance and publication, regulation and licensing, and the closing of the theatres. Part II, by Gerald Bentley, covers the private and public theatres and the history of the various companies of actors from the King's Men down, from 1613 to 1642. Part III, by Kathleen McLuskie, deals with playwrights from 1613 to 1642, including Thomas Heywood, John Fletcher, Philip Massinger, John Ford, William Davenant, Ben Jonson, Richard Brome, and James Shirley. Part IV, by Lois Potter, continues Part III from 1642 to 1660, covering Killigrew, the Duchess of Newcastle, John Tatham, William Davenant, and others. This collection does not systematically consider Shakespeare during the period but does identify the conditions of theatre and performance in which revivals of his plays continued to figure, as partly illustrated in G. Taylor and J. Jowett, *Shakespeare Reshaped 1606–1623* (1993). Fuller coverage of the drama's political contexts appears in M. Butler, *Theatre and Crisis, 1632–1642* (1984).

156. **Hazlitt, William C., ed.** *The English Drama and Stage Under the Tudor and Stuart Princes 1543–1664 Illustrated by a Series of Documents, Treatises and Poems.* [Edinburgh?]: Roxborough Library, 1869.

Hazlitt includes government documents relating to the stage, dealing with performances, plays, actors, theatres, and such topics as the closing of theatres in 1642. He reprints treatises attacking and defending the theatre, such as the ironic protest to Phoebus about the closing of the theatres; Richard Flecknoe's short *Discourse of the English Stage* (1660); and other sources of theatrical data. This anthology of 17th-century texts shows the practices of and attitudes to the English Renaissance theatre.

157. **Leggatt, Alexander.** *Jacobean Public Theatre.* London and New York: Routledge, 1992.

Leggatt seeks to evoke the conditions of the Jacobean public theatres from 1603 to 1625, considering theatre structures, audiences, scripts, and staging. Part of the book considers how the 1608 quarto of *Lear* would work in the Globe Theatre, using evidence from audience effect, props, costumes, and other visual clues. Particular attention is given to the imaginative appeal of the eccentricities of the Fool and Edgar.

See also nos. 14, 20, 30, 31, 32, 36, 67, 69, 72, 105, 106, 111a, 125, 126, 133, 140, 150.

C. THE INTERREGNUM: 1660–1837

1. General Studies

158. **Archer, William, and Robert W. Lowe, eds.** *Dramatic Essays.* 3 vols. London: Walter Scott, 1895.

This collection contains selected reviews and essays about performances by Leigh Hunt (on the Kembles, Siddons, Pope, Jordan), William Hazlitt (on Booth, Kemble, Macready), John Forster (on Macready, Forrest, Kean), and George Lewes (on Macready versus Kean as Shylock, and on Kean's other Shakespearean roles). The selections provide overlapping commentaries about performers in the earlier 19th-century theatre, mostly devoted to Shakespeare.

159. **Avery, Emmett, and Charles B. Hogan.** *The London Stage: A Calendar of Plays, Entertainments and Afterpieces, 1660–1800.* 11 Vols. Carbondale: Univ. of Southern Illinois Press, 1960–65.

This chronological listing of productions provides preliminary data for one major segment of Shakespearean performance history, including play titles and authors, performance locales, dates, and cast (where known), plus brief notes on provenance of adaptations, etc.

160. **Branam, George C.** *Eighteenth Century Adaptations of Shakespearean Tragedy.* Berkeley: Univ. of California Press, 1956.

Branam describes and explains the aesthetics of the 18th-century Shakespeare adaptors, with detailed reference to specific adaptations. He covers I) Alterations; II) Influence of Critical Theory and the Neoclassic Rules: Unities, Decorum, Verisimilitude,

Poetical Justice, Didacticism; III) Language: Clarity, Prosody, Puns, Elevation, Reduction of Imagery; IV) Character and Moral (consistency is stressed); V) Stage Effectiveness: Action and Report, Spectacle and Song, Female Interest, Endings. He includes a bibliography and an appendix with a check-list of Shakespearean adaptations 1660–1820. The book provides a positive overview, not intensively developed. A more recent study in this field is J. Marsden, *The Re-Imagined Text: Shakespeare, Adaptation and Eighteenth Century Literary Theory* (1995).

161. **Davis, Thomas.** *Dramatic Miscellanies Consisting of Critical Observations on Several Plays of Shakespeare: With a Review of his Principal Characters, and those of the various eminent writers as represented by Mr. Garrick and other celebrated Comedians with anecdotes of Dramatic Poets, Actors, etc.* Dublin: S. Price, H. Whitestone, etc., 1784.

Davis gives an exhaustive account, particularly at Covent Garden, with lists and detailed observations about the characters, texts, and performances of about a third of Shakespeare's plays. He notes such details as various *Lears* including Garrick's (from which current taste forced Garrick to exclude the Fool). He also discusses Ben Jonson at length, mentions many other dramatists, and concludes with essays on Betterton and Cibber, including discussion of the political use of *Henry IV* against Walpole. This book is a repository of first-hand observations about 17th- and 18th-century Shakespearean productions.

162. **Donohue, Joseph W.,** *Dramatic Character in the English Romantic Age.* Princeton: Princeton Univ. Press, 1970.

Chapter I of Part I contrasts the influence of the drama of Shakespeare and of Fletcher in the 17th century. Part III covers Shakespearean characterization in the Romantic age with Chapter VIII about the characterization of Macbeth and Richard III; Chapter IX on Garrick's Shakespeare and subjective dramatic character; Chapter X on Kemble, his performance of Macbeth with Mrs. Siddons, and on George Cooke; Chapter XII on Kean's roles as Richard III and Macbeth, with Hazlitt's commentary. Part II deals with other authors reflecting a similar evolution in Romantic characterization to that seen in Shakespeare productions. There are 49 illustrations.

163. **Doran, Dr. J[ohn].** *"Their Majesties' Servants" or Annals of the English Stage from Thomas Betterton to Edmund Kean: Actors, Authors, Audiences.* London: John C. Nimms, 1863.

Among many other topics and performers, Doran's illustrated survey covers "boy-actresses" and their female successors, Thomas Betterton, Elizabeth Barry, 17th- and 18th-century audiences, James Quinn, Barton Booth, David Garrick, Pegg Woffington, Colley Cibber, Samuel Foote, Sarah Siddons, John Kemble, and Edmund Kean. The book is discursive, gossipy, anecdotal, detailed, and encyclopedic.

164. **Downes, J.** *Roscius Anglicanus, or, an Historical Review of the Stage.* 1708. Ed. Montague Summers, London: Fortune, 1928.

The 1708 edition is subtitled: "or an Historical Review of the Stage After it had been Suppressed by means of the late Unhappy Civil War, begun in 1641, till the Time of King Charles the II's Restoration in May, 1660. Giving an Account of its Rise again; of the Time and Places, the Governors of both the Companies first Erected their Theatres. The Names of the Principal Actors and Actresses who Performed in the Chiefest Plays in each House. With the Names of the most taking Plays; and Modern Poets. For the space of 46 years. . .1660, to 1706." The reprint is a facsimile of Downes' erratic recollections as book-keeper and prompter to Davenant's company (with Betterton), covering the continuities from Shakespeare's company to Davenant's, reflected in many of his Shakespearean revivals (*Macbeth, Lear, Tempest, Timon, Merry Wives,* etc.). He also includes much gossip, such as Pepys' comment on the superiority of Kynaston's charms in female roles to those of women in his audiences. This is a key source, with over two hundred pages of useful notes in Summers' edition (e.g., giving relevant Pepys references), plus the text of *A Satyr upon the Players*, with contemporary references to Restoration actors. A recent edition is J. Downes, *Roscius Anglicanus*, eds. J. Milhous and R. D. Hume (1987).

165. **Genest, John.** *Some Account of the English Stage from the Restoration in 1660 to 1830.* 10 vols. Bath: H. E. Carrington, 1832.

This combined chronicle and calendar of London and provincial performances contains an encyclopedic range of contemporary information and elaborate commentary about productions, theatres, actors, and scripts, consolidating innumerable earlier sources covering 170 years. While anecdotal and subject to correction by more recent research and adjustment to match changes of taste, it remains a valuable source of performance data, frequently with direct relevance to the history of Shakespeare production (though the indexes of this edition are inadequate).

166. **Gray, Charles H.** *Theatrical Criticism in London to 1795.* New York: Columbia Univ. Press, 1931.

This survey identifies sources in newspapers, journals, and magazines from which to derive 18th-century theatrical criticism. It traces development of performance criticism into a professional mode of analysis from Shakespeare's time to 1795, with citations on performances (especially of Shakespeare). It shows how theatre reviews reflect artistic assumptions and prejudices of the time, such as the neoclassical doctrine of "the Unities." The titles referred to suggest avenues for further research. There is an index of publications, play-titles, dramatists, and actors, but only a one-page bibliography. Publication dates are cited, but footnotes are minimal and access to sources is not established. For the newspaper collections on which Gray draws, he refers scholars to R. S. Crane and F. B. Kaye, *A Census of British Newspapers and Periodicals, 1620–1800* (1927). Gray's book has many original aperçus. For example, 18th-century aesthetic values are memorably illustrated by Gray's recovery (196) of John Potter's censure of *Richard III* because "parts are trifling, others shocking, and some improbable," and of Potter's praise of the propriety of Tate's happy ending to *Lear*.

167. **Highfill, Philip, Jr., Kalman A. Burnim, and Edward A. Langhans.** *A Biographical Dictionary of Actors, Actresses, Musicians, and Other Stage Personnel in London, 1660–1800.* 16 vols. Carbondale: Southern Illinois Univ. Press, 1973–93.

This illustrated alphabetical list provides detailed accounts of the careers and biographies of all recorded theatre personnel from the reopening of the theatres to 1800. It often includes detailed contemporary accounts of Shakespeare performances: e.g., of Sarah Siddons playing Lady Macbeth, Desdemona, Queen Elizabeth (*Richard III*), and Queen Katherine (*Henry VIII*). The 67 pages about Siddons list and describe 387 portraits, paintings, and memorabilia of her. Garrick receives 103 pages with a list of 250 such items. Even obscure careers are recorded. The early 18th-century portrayal of the Old Lady in *Henry VIII* by an actress called Mrs. Willis can be located in the fifty-year career of Mrs. Elizabeth Willis (among several women called Willis).

168. **Hogan, Charles B.** *Shakespeare in the Theatre: A Record of Performances in London, 1701–1800.* 2 Vols. Oxford: Clarendon Press, 1952–57.

The first part of this calendar chronicles every identifiable performance by year and theatre, drawing on any available source. The second part covers the plays' cast lists and other surviving data, often extensive, drawn from newspapers, playbills, promptbooks, and published scripts (such as Thomas Shadwell's *Timon*, Dryden's *Troilus*, and Otway's *Romeo*). Appendices cover the number of performances of Shakespeare's plays in order of popularity, and a listing of London theatres of the period. The material is useful for tracing the standing and treatment of Shakespearean scripts during a period when performances were affected by drastic revision of Shakespeare's text. The principal theatres used are described by R. Southern, *The Georgian Playhouse* (1948).

169. **Hotson, Leslie.** *The Commonwealth and Restoration Stage.* Cambridge, Mass.: Harvard Univ. Press, 1928.

Hotson draws on legal records from 120 suits relating to theatres and actors from 1635 to 1704. Section I deals with Players and Parliament (Surreptitious Drama, 1642–1655; Bear Gardens). Section II surveys Playhouses (Red Bull, Phoenix, Salisbury Court; Gibbon and Lisle's Tennis Courts). Section III deals with Davenant's "Opera," 1655–1660. Section IV covers George Jolly and the Nursery Theatre. Section V documents the Duke's Company, 1660–1682. Section VI is concerned with the King's Company,

1660–1682. Section VII covers the United Company, 1682–1694. Section VIII groups together the Rival Companies, 1695–1704. Hotson shows that performance of plays persisted through the Commonwealth by citing exact legal data including financial accounts. An Appendix reprints relevant Chancery Bills and Answers, etc. Hotson strengthens the case for continuity from Shakespeare's time to the Restoration theatre.

170. **Howe, Elizabeth.** *The First English Actresses: Women and Drama 1660–1700.* Cambridge: Cambridge Univ. Press, 1992.

This account of the first forty years of actresses performing on the English stage discusses professional conditions, including decorum and sexuality on and off stage. The author shows that Nell Gwyn's roles in witty comedy (such as *Much Ado*) suggest sexual parity, while Elizabeth Barry's roles in tragedy are seen as limiting women, who are either angels or devils. She uses prologues and epilogues as documentary evidence for these observations. Much relates to Shakespearean performance, such as the first appearance on the English stage of an actress playing Shakespeare late in 1660 (perhaps as Desdemona, on 8 December 1660). Thereafter she sees an increase in sentimentality, as shown by Tate's alteration in Cordelia's role. These early actresses are set in a fuller chronological context down to the present in R. Findlater, *The Player Queens* (1977). See also J. A. Roberts. "Shakespearean Comedy and Some Eighteenth-Century Actresses." In K. Muir, J. Halio, and D. J. Palmer eds., *Shakespeare: Man of the Theatre*, 212–30 (1983).

171. **Odell, George C.D.** *Shakespeare from Betterton to Irving.* 2 vols. New York: Charles Scribner's, 1920. Repr. with new Introduction by Robert H. Ball, New York: Dover, 1966.

This encyclopedic account (with illustrations) of the treatment of Shakespeare from 1660 to 1902 is broken into sections devoted to the times of Betterton; Cibber; Garrick; Kemble; the interregnum of 1817–37; Macready; Phelps and Charles Kean; and Irving. Each section covers the buildings with their regulation and operation; the current principles and specifics of scenery, staging, and costumes; and the handling and performance of scripts. The chronicle is selective in depth of coverage, concentrating almost exclusively on London, but it is informative as an overview of theatrical practices, including contemporary critical comment and background about specific major performances. The account provides plausible interpretations of theatrical records and their implications, though its aesthetic judgments and commentary now seem over-confident and more detailed local studies make parts no longer current. Further details about Shakespearean productions appear incidentally in George C. D. Odell, *Annals of the New York Stage* (1927). See also R. Findlater. *The Player Kings* (1971).

172. **Schoester, Robert.** *United States Theatre: A Bibliography from the Beginning to 1990.* Romsey, U.K.: Motley Press, 1993.

This comprehensive bibliography is concerned exclusively with the British theatrical tradition in the U.S.A. Its categories include Section A: Theatre (federal and state stages; their locations; religious theatre; theatre clubs and societies; theatre biographies, including critics; reviews, vaudevilles, and showboats; community and university theatres); Section B: Drama (plays from 1665–1990: general play lists, publishing, theory, history, international views and influence, author biographies and related criticism); Section C: Music (the musical, and play music); Section D: Indexes (by subject and author). Entries cover books, pamphlets, and theses only, excluding journal articles. Publication references identify authors, texts, plates, publishers, places, and dates, followed by brief descriptive notes. This unusual book provides a thorough and current source of writing about the British theatre tradition in the U.S.A., with its massive Shakespearean component.

173. **Spencer, Hazelton,** *Shakespeare Improved: The Restoration Versions in Quarto and on the Stage.* Cambridge, Mass.: Harvard Univ. Press 1927.

Spencer reviews Shakespeare performances in London, 1660–1710. Part I gives the stage history of the plays; Part II covers the adaptations of Davenant, Dryden, Tate, miscellaneous others, and unaltered quarto versions (*Othello, Henry IV*, and *Caesar)*. An Appendix lists public theatres and companies appearing in them from 1660 to 1710. Bibliographies cite first editions of altered versions; general studies of these versions; studies of single plays; and works on Restoration Theatre. Though predating much later research, this survey is comprehensive and detailed. The aesthetics involved are discussed in M. Dobson, *The Making of a National Poet: Shakespeare, Adaptation & Authorship, 1660–1769* (1992). Some relevant Restoration scripts are reprinted with commentaries in *Shakespeare Adaptations: "The Tempest," "The Mock Tempest," and "King Lear,"* ed. M. Summers (1922); and *Five Restoration Adaptations of Shakespeare*, ed. C. Spencer (1965), including Davenant's *Macbeth*, Dryden's *Tempest*, Tate's *Lear*, Cibber's *Richard III*, and Granville's *Jew of Venice*.

174. **Wright, James.** *Historia Histrionica: An Historical Account of the English Stage Shewing The ancient Use, Improvement & Perfection of Dramatic Representations, in this Nation in a Dialogue of Plays and Players.* London: G. Croon, 1699. Facsimile reprint. London: Ashee Facsimiles, 1872.

Wright records the characteristics of 17th-century English drama, including pre-Civil War theatre, with notes on Lowin, Taylor, and Pollard; the Blackfriars Theatre; boys in women's roles; Elizabethan and Jacobean theatrical decorum, as judged by Dryden's neoclassicism; censorship; Restoration acting and earlier styles; etc. Wright is a useful if uneven early source about 17th-century theatre practices.

See also nos. 126, 130, 131, 133, 134, 139, 140, 144, 146, 147.

2. Individual Managers and Actors

175. **Ashley, Leonard R. N.** *Colley Cibber.* New York: Twayne, 1965.

Ashley gives a succinct overview of the career of a major actor-manager. Chapters include the Actor; Playwright; Management; Drury Lane and its company; and the *Apology*. The book has a chronology and a bibliography. It is slighter but more current than R. H. Barker's *Mr. Cibber of Drury Lane* (1939). The original autobiographical source for these studies remains Colley Cibber, *An Apology for the Life of Mr. Colley Cibber* (1740), edited R. W. Dent

(1914), in which Cibber incidentally surveys the work of most of his contemporaries in the English theatre from 1660 onwards. See also C. Cibber, *An Apology for the Life of Mr. Colley Cibber*, ed. B. R. S. Fone (1968).

176. **Baker, Herschel.** *John Philip Kemble: The Actor in his Theatre.* New York: Greenwood Press, 1969.

This biography stresses the attempts at authenticity of staging in such Kemble revivals as *Henry VIII* (1788) with his sister Sarah Siddons as Queen Katherine, and also notes his successes as Hamlet and Coriolanus among other roles. In surveying Kemble's numerous Shakespeare revivals, it demonstrates that Kemble hacked the texts drastically, even while showing why Odell calls him the first great producer of Shakespeare. Baker notes Kemble's success in *Macbeth* with a merely imagined Ghost of Banquo, and his equal success with the history plays resulting from his regal stateliness of acting style, in which he challenged his livelier rival, Cooke. The book ends with a useful bibliography, including such important early precedents as J. Boaden, *Memoirs of the Life of John Philip Kemble* (1825); and P. Fitzgerald, *The Kembles* (1871).

177. **Downer, Alan S.** *The Eminent Tragedian, William Charles Macready.* Cambridge, Mass.: Harvard Univ. Press, 1966.

This biography uses Macready's diary, promptbooks, and contemporary reviews to detail his career, with accounts of his many major Shakespeare roles, including Richard III, Macbeth, and Othello. Downer provides exact production data about such performances, and he describes Macready's concern with ensuring the "correctness" of his productions in terms of scripts, costumes, design, and consistency. His rigorous discipline in training actors is also established here, and he applied it to himself: he wore his armor for *Henry V* at home to make it familiar. Much of the Shakespearean material comes from *Macready's Reminiscences and Selections from his Diaries and Letters*, ed. F. Pollock (1875).

178. **Edmond, Mary.** *Rare Sir William Davenant.* Manchester: Manchester Univ. Press, 1987.

This account of the career of Davenant describes the evolution of

English theatre during the 17th century, under the influence of ideas and aesthetics from France and Italy such as the doctrines of the neo-Aristotelean unities and the separation of genres. Edmond explains that, while first associated closely with Shakespeare's own company before the Commonwealth, from the Restoration Davenant was a leader in adjusting Shakespearean scripts and performances to the new aesthetic, with the assistance of his distinguished theatre company led by Thomas Betterton and newly accepted actresses such as Mrs. Betterton. Edmond gives an exact account of the sophisticated devices, scenery, and other resources of the newly built and tightly regulated theatres. She shows how this leading manager of the Restoration drastically elaborated the English performance tradition in ways still accepted by most modern theatre professionals, unaccustomed to the simple permanent stages of Elizabethan theatres. Further sources are listed in S. B. Blaydes and P. Bordinat, *Sir William Davenant: An Annotated Bibliography 1629–1985* (1986).

179. **FitzSimmons, Raymond.** *Edmund Kean: Fire from Heaven.* New York: Dial, 1976.

This illustrated biography of a leading Shakespearean actor also includes much material on Kean's contemporaries who shared Kean's Shakespearean interests: Macready, Kemble, etc. The book describes in some detail Kean's greatest roles: Shylock, Richard III, Othello, and Iago. it updates even such comprehensive earlier studies as H. N. Hillebrand, *Edmund Kean* (1933). However, the customary responses to Kean's intensity in these roles recorded in such studies can perhaps be attributed to new lighting techniques, possibly reinforced by the drug-taking of the Romantic critics, according to T. C. Davis, "'Reading Shakespeare by Flashes of Lightning': Challenging the Foundations of Romantic Acting Theory," *English Literary History* 62: 933–54.

180. **Gildon, Charles.** *The Life of Mr. Thomas Betterton.* London: Robert Gosling, 1710.

This discussion of acting techniques takes the form of a platonic dialogue in which Gildon records Betterton's "Discourse of Acting," reported from the last year of his life, in which acting is defended as next to preaching and law in moral significance.

Betterton's procedures and professional rigor are established, with his criteria for legitimate performance, which offer a professional code for the Restoration theatre, and a baseline for discussion and evaluation of later developments in acting and staging, including gesture and facial expression. The values of propriety, decorum, and discipline follow the precedent of Hamlet's advice to the players. The book covers the work of individual actors and actresses such as Mrs. Barry, and includes St. Evremond's views on theatrical music and dance. Despite the book's contrived format, it provides a documentary account of professional theatre practices and values in the neoclassical period of English drama.

181. **Hazlitt, William.** *Criticism and Dramatic Essays of the English Stage.* London: G. Routledge, 1851.

Hazlitt's discussions center on the roles of Edmund Kean, especially Richard III, Iago, Macbeth, Lear, Coriolanus, Richard II, Romeo, and Hamlet. The book starts with general essays on the theatre: actors, comedy, poetry, critics, opera, popular art, etc. While his style is journalistic and conversational, not scholarly, Hazlitt's writing is sensible and precise, and it evokes the theatre of his time vividly, particularly its productions of Shakespeare. See also W. Hazlitt, *Art and Dramatic Criticism.* In *The Complete Works*, ed. P. P. Howe (1930).

182. **Hunt, Leigh.** *Leigh Hunt's Dramatic Criticism 1808–1831.* Ed. Lawrence H. Houtchens and Carolyn W. Houtchens. New York: Columbia Univ. Press, 1949.

This anthology includes substantial reviews of performances of *Lear* (rejecting Tate's version), *Much Ado, John, Twelfth Night, Caesar, Othello, Richard III, Timon, Romeo,* and *Coriolanus.* There are significant analyses of Kean's *Richard III* versus Macready's, of Kemble's *Henry VIII*, and of Sarah Siddons' career. This book covers a cross-section of early 19th-century Shakespeare performances.

183. **Kemble, John Philip.** *Promptbooks.* Ed. Charles Shattuck. 10 vols. Washington D. C. (Folger Library): Univ. of Virginia Press, 1974.

Shattuck reprints the texts of Shakespeare's plays owned by

Kemble and staged by him. In developing his productions Kemble lightly marked each script to indicate interpretational and practical procedures to be used in his productions, so his notations provide authentic contemporary clues about these productions, which are interpreted in H. Child, *The Shakespeare Productions of John Philip Kemble* (1935).

184. **Kendall, Alan.** *David Garrick: A Biography.* London: Harrap, 1985.

In this fully illustrated account, Kendall seeks to interpret the personality of Garrick, not just to chronicle the career. He makes searching use of primary and secondary material, paying particular attention to the inward life reflected in Garrick's letters. In its more incisive approach, the book provides a deliberate contrast and complement to the data in the biography by G. W. Stone and G. M. Kahrl, *David Garrick: A Critical Biography* (1979). Fuller production details appear in K. A. Burnim, *David Garrick, Director* (1961).

185. **Manvell, Roger.** *Sarah Siddons: Portrait of an Actress.* London: Heinemann, 1971.

This full biography provides an overview of Siddons' theatrical career and personality, with some attention to her portrayal of such major roles as Lady Macbeth and Queen Katherine (*Henry VIII*). There are sixty illustrations; appendices listing Siddons' roles and citing Bell's notes on her Lady Macbeth; a Select Bibliography; and an Index of Plays and Parts in which Sarah Siddons appeared. Her Shakespeare roles are often mentioned but are not stressed, as they are in Yvonne Ffrench, *Mrs. Siddons: Tragic Actress* (1936, revised 1954). See no. 176.

See also nos. 126, 133, 134, 144, 147, 158, 159, 160, 161, 163, 164, 165, 166, 167, 168, 171, 172, 173, 174, 188.

D. Modern Performances: 1837–1998

1. General Studies

186. **Beauman, Sally.** *The Royal Shakespeare Company: A History of Ten Decades.* Oxford: Oxford Univ. Press, 1982.

Beauman chronicles the first century of the history of the acting companies based at theatres in Stratford-upon-Avon since 1879. The early phases illustrate characteristic problems of actor-managers like Frank Benson in creating a tradition, facilities, and an audience. The account describes struggles to rebuild the fire-struck theatre in the twenties, and the modern florescence of the company as a multi-theatre group, including London, with international standing, through the innovations of Peter Brook, Peter Hall, and Trevor Nunn, among others. Beauman explains this progress through policy, funding, administration, facilities, production characteristics, individual performances, and responses of audiences and critics. Such a broad perspective limits attention to individual interpretations, though illuminating detail is provided, with many illustrations. This book supersedes R. Ellis, *The Shakespeare Memorial Theatre* (1948), as Beauman establishes the context for more exact analyses of specific artistic achievements, but Ellis has 93 photographs.

187. **Billington, Michael.** *Peggy Ashcroft.* London: John Murray, 1988. Revised, London: Mandarin, 1991.

Written by a leading London theatre critic, this biography of a prominent British 20th-century actress surveys a career largely devoted to Shakespearean roles, and one closely associated with the Old Vic, the Shakespeare Memorial Theatre at Stratford-upon-Avon, and the Royal Shakespeare Company. While primarily devoted to an individual career, the book also notes key aspects of significant productions. It describes Ashcroft's initial performance as Juliet; her Beatrice in Gielgud's *Much Ado*; and her climactic triumph as Queen Margaret in the R.S.C. cycle, *The Wars of the Roses*, based on Shakespeare's history plays, and directed by Hall and Barton (1963–64). There is much detail about leading directors, costumes, staging, and the reception of numerous productions. While no single production is treated exhaustively, the biography documents how one individual's experience of modern technical and stylistic changes in the professional theatre affected Shakespeare productions.

188. **Carlisle, Carol Jones.** *Shakespeare from the Greenroom: Actors' Criticisms of Four Major Tragedies.* Chapel Hill: Univ. of North Carolina Press, 1969.

This survey draws chiefly on leading theatrical figures such as Garrick, Granville-Barker, and Gielgud, to provide "an account of the best Shakespearean criticisms by English and American actors past and present" (vii). It "deals with plays as plays: with the characters as personalities to be projected in action on a stage; with language as something to be spoken" (viii). It surveys *Hamlet, Othello, Lear,* and *Macbeth*, under two broad headings: "The Play" and "The Characters." Each of these two topics is broken down into smaller categories relevant to the particular script. The *Hamlet* section on the play covers plot, theatrical effectiveness, language, and meaning. It is followed by characterizations of Hamlet (his age, his madness, his relations with his mother), of Gertrude, of Claudius, etc. In the *Othello* section on characters, Carlisle discusses the hero's blackness of complexion. *Lear*, the play, covers adaptations like Tate's, setting, actability, etc. Among *Macbeth*'s characters, she includes the supernatural figures, as developed in Davenant's version. The review of the character of Lady Macbeth contrasts Mrs. Siddons' interpretation to her actual performance. Carlisle's selection favors prominent interpreters, and she often refers to their performances as well as to their formal criticism.

189. **Cohn, Ruby.** *Modern Shakespeare Offshoots.* Princeton: Princeton Univ. Press, 1976.

Rather than modern productions reinterpreting standard scripts, Cohn surveys radical revisions, mostly of four Shakespeare plays, *Macbeth, Hamlet, Lear,* and *Tempest*, during the last century and a half, concentrating on versions in English, French, and German. She notes earlier reconstructions of the English Restoration, and of the German and French Romantics (such as Goethe and

Laforgue). There are chapters on twentieth-century reconstructions by Shaw, Brecht, Beckett, with allusions to Hauptmann, Welles, Marowitz, Papp, etc. The book casts light on patterns of modern Shakespeare production through Cohn's exploration of intellectual contexts of specific authors, scripts, and productions. Her contrasts between originals and adaptations are illuminating.

190. **Crosse, Gordon.** *Shakespearean Playgoing, 1890–1952.* London: A. R. Mowbray, 1953.

In this revision of an earlier text (1940), Crosse offers a selective, personal, and comparative survey of major theatre figures in his lifetime: Irving, Benson, Old Vic managers, Terry, Gielgud, Thorndike, Laughton, Guinness, Bloom, Wolfit, Welles, etc. Through selective detail from individual productions, he displays the shift in production values from Tree's elaborate staging, through the revived Elizabethan staging, to use of modern dress and other "eccentricities" of Guthrie and his contemporaries. The values are old-fashioned, but there is much first-hand data, including seventeen photographs.

191. **Granville-Barker, Harley.** *Prefaces to Shakespeare.* 2 Vols. Princeton: Princeton Univ. Press, 1946–47. *More Prefaces to Shakespeare,* 1974.

These prefaces have frequently been reprinted in various formats, since they were originally written in the nineteen-twenties for an unpublished edition by Ernest Benn Ltd. to be called *The Players' Shakespeare.* They reflect the author's experience as a leading actor and director of Shakespeare, himself a playwright rather than a scholar. In the 1946–47 volumes, he considers interpretations and staging relevant to actual productions of *Love's Labour's, Romeo, Merchant, Caesar, Hamlet, Othello, Lear, Antony, Coriolanus,* and *Cymbeline.* The 1974 volume considers *Dream, Winter's Tale, Twelfth Night, Macbeth,* and *Henry V,* with the Preface for the original Player's Shakespeare. The Prefaces reflect the performance values seen in Granville-Barker's own celebrated productions of *Winter's Tale, Twelfth Night,* and *Dream.* A detailed account of the Prefaces' relation to Granville-Barker's work with the professional theatre appears in Dennis Kennedy, *Granville-Barker and the*

Dream of Theatre (1985), which shows that these performances were uncut, rapid, spare, and largely followed Poel's devotion to simplified Elizabethan staging shared with Granville-Barker's other mentor, Ben Greet.

192. **Hill, Errol.** *Shakespeare in Sable: A History of Black Shakespearean Actors.* Amherst: Univ. Massachusetts Press, 1984.

Hill is a Trinidadian trained in theatre in both the U.K. and the U.S.A. He surveys the careers of black actors of Shakespeare, chiefly in America, paying attention to the overtly African roles of Aaron the Moor, the Prince of Morocco, Othello, and Cleopatra. Hill describes the historical effects of black casting on predominantly white audiences in the course of narrating the careers of relevant actors, companies, and productions in the 19th and 20th centuries, from the ill-fated New York African Company and the movement to England of Ira Aldridge, Morgan Smith, and Paul Molyneaux. He documents the resurgence of American black theatre after the Civil War, fostering such careers as those of Charles Wood and Henrietta Davis. He shows its decline in the early 20th century, until its flowering in the Federal Theatre Project, with Welles' *Macbeth*. Thereafter, Hill shows how the career of Paul Robeson established precedents for recognition of black Shakespeareans; and how, from 1953, Joseph Papp fostered multiracial approaches and color-blind casting, both of which this book advocates.

193. **Jacobs, Henry E., and Claudia Johnson.** *An Annotated Bibliography of Shakespeare Burlesques, Parodies, and Travesties.* New York: Garland, 1976.

This catalogue of printed texts covers plays, scenes, and passages related to Shakespeare, showing popular responses and emphases. The book lists subjects alphabetically by Shakespeare titles, or as independent plays and collections, and it gives authors, titles, publication data, Library of Congress catalogue numbers, and summaries of content. Relevant scripts are provided by *Nineteenth-Century Shakespeare Burlesques*, ed. S. Wells (1977).

194. **Kemp, Thomas C.** *Birmingham Repertory Theatre: The Playhouse and the Man.* Birmingham: Cornish, 1948.

Kemp surveys the Birmingham company's history as one of the leading provincial U.K. repertory groups during the period 1907–47, including the career of Barry Jackson in it from 1913 to 1946. He shows how it rivaled nearby Stratford-upon-Avon because of the numerous Shakespearean plays it staged, including such distinctive productions as modern-dress versions of *Cymbeline* (1923), *Hamlet* (1925), *Othello* (1928), and *The Taming of the Shrew* (1942).

195. **Kennedy, Dennis.** *Looking at Shakespeare: A Visual History of Twentieth-Century Performance.* Cambridge: Cambridge Univ. Press, 1993.

This scholarly overview elucidates changes in pictorial production values from Charles Kean's historical documentary approach in the 19th century, followed by the revolution of Gordon Craig, Harley Granville-Barker, and Max Reinhardt, down to the postmodern effects in the work of Peter Brook, Peter Hall, Michael Kahn, Peter Zadek, and Michael Bogdanov. It also examines the visual ideas and scenic effects of productions by William Poel, Tyrone Guthrie, Bertolt Brecht, and other innovators. It covers the German and Italian stage, with Giorgio Strehler's *Tempest* at the Teatro Lyrico of Milan. The 171 illustrations establish 20th-century performance values.

196. **Kolin, Philip C., ed.** *Shakespeare in the South: Essays in Performance.* Jackson, Miss.: University Press of Mississippi, 1983.

Some essays in this anthology survey early Shakespeare performances in southern states: Virginia, 1751–1863 (Arnold Aronson); Maryland, 1752–1860 (Christopher J. Thais); and Mississippi, 1814–1980 (Linwood E. Orange). Others focus on cities: Charleston, 1764–1799 (Sarah Nalley) and 1800–1860 (Woodrow L. Holbein); New Orleans, 1817–1865 (Joseph P. Rapollo); Mobile, 1822–1861 (Mary D. Toulmin); and Houston, 1839–1980 (Waldo McNeir). Charles B. Lower reviews treatments of Othello as a Black on Southern stages. Modern festivals in several Southern states are covered: in North Carolina (Larry Champion);

in Birmingham, Alabama (Carol M. Kay); in Odessa, Texas (Earl L. Dachlager); and in Orlando, Florida (Stuart E. Omans and Patricia A. Madden). Kolin shows how the South attracted actors such as Edmund Kean, William Macready, Edwin Booth, Charlotte Cushman, and Richard Dreyfuss. Kolin provides one regional perspective of Shakespeare's role in the American theatre.

197. **Mullin, Michael, with Karen Morris Muriello.** *Theatre at Stratford-upon-Avon: A Catalogue-Index of the Shakespeare Memorial/Royal Shakespeare Theatre, 1879–1978.* 2 Vols. Westport, Conn.: Greenwood Press, 1980.

This reference index covers archives of the Shakespeare Centre Library, Stratford-upon-Avon, U.K., providing a full record, including promptbooks and reviews, for most Stratford productions since the 1879 opening of the Shakespeare Memorial Theatre. Volume 1: Catalogue of Productions; Volume 2: Indexes and Calendar. The productions include those at successive theatres in Stratford (with the Other Place) and the London theatre of the Royal Shakespeare Company, the Aldwych. After an historical survey of the general directors of the successive companies, the first volume lists plays produced by title, citing the author, translator (if any), director, designer, light-designer (if known), cast, and British reviews in the archives. Volume 2 has an index of playwrights, with titles of their plays and dates of the plays' opening performances; an index of theatre personnel (directors, designers, actors) with relevant titles and dates for each; an index of reviewers, with titles and productions covered; and a calendar of productions. While the index is best used in the archives at Stratford (copied at the University of Illinois), this text helps with library files of British newspapers; actors' and directors' biographies; and theatre surveys on modern productions of Shakespeare originating in Stratford.

198. **Rowell, George.** *The Old Vic Theatre: A History.* Cambridge: Cambridge Univ. Press, 1993.

This illustrated chronological survey provides an overview of the administration of the Old Vic from its inception, with some notice of productions. Shakespeare figures prominently in Chapter 5: "Seeking Shakespeare 1914–1933," which covers Ben Greet,

Robert Atkins, and Harcourt Williams; and Chapter 6 discusses Tyrone Guthrie. There are references to Edith Evans and similar stars. Appendices list plays performed at the Old Vic, including many by Shakespeare. A rather more production-oriented account is given in P. Roberts, *The Old Vic Story: A Nation's Theatre 1818–1976* (1976). Descriptions of two of the Old Vic's most productive periods, from 1934 to 1947, and from 1947 to 1957, are given in A. Williamson, *Old Vic Drama: A Twelve Years' Study of Plays and Players* (1947) and *Old Vic Drama 2: 1947–1957* (1957). See also one director's perspective in H. Williams, *Old Vic Saga* (1949). Another Old Vic Shakespeare director in the later period discusses his productions there from 1949 to 1953 in H. Hunt, *Old Vic Prefaces* (1954). Five later annuals (1953 to 1957) edited variously by R. Wood, M. Clarke, A. McBean, H. Rogers, and P. Chandler, provide cast lists, photographs and reviews: *Shakespeare at the Old Vic* (1954–58).

199. **Wearing, J. P. ed.** *The London Stage: A Calendar of Plays and Players, 1890–1959.* 15 vols. Metuchen, N. J.: Scarecrow Press, 1976–84.

This chronological series of playbills for the principal London theatres provides script-titles, plays' genre and number of acts, authors, dates, lengths and numbers of performances, casts, production staffs, short bibliographies of first-night reviews, and comments. Indexes follow the relevant ten-year periods covered by each of seven groups of volumes, into which the whole period is broken down. The entries document major London productions of Shakespeare for a significant period.

See also nos. 125, 128, 130, 131, 133, 134, 139, 140, 144, 146, 147, 148, 152, 158.

2. The Victorians and Edwardians: 1837–1914

200. **Allen, Shirley S.** *Samuel Phelps and the Sadler's Wells Theatre.* Middletown, Conn.: Wesleyan Univ. Press, 1971.

This biography of a leading actor and director shows how he achieved major reforms: he integrated the stage effects in his productions of Shakespeare, including noteworthy revivals of neglected plays; he avoided "stars," stressing minor characters and fresh lighting effects (e.g., for ghosts in *Hamlet* and *Richard III*); he adopted a classic repertory not supported by aristocratic society, but appealing to large audiences (2,600) at low ticket prices in the pit. The book includes detailed accounts of Macready and Kean. Allen argues that Phelps first restored the original Shakespeare scripts for such plays as *Macbeth, Lear,* and *Richard III,* and that he revived *Antony* and *Pericles.* She suggests that he anticipated the Method by his development of consistency and sincerity of characterization in such roles as Iago, Leontes, Timon, and Brutus. See also D. Arundell, *The Story of Sadler's Wells 1683–1964* (1965).

201. **Craig, Edward.** *Gordon Craig.* New York: Alfred A. Knopf, 1968.

This detailed biography of Edward Gordon Craig, son of the actress Ellen Terry and a revolutionary set designer, places Craig's stage designs in their full social, theatrical, and artistic contexts, covering the climactic Shakespearean project of the Moscow *Hamlet* in Chapter 12. It shows the influence of Craig on theatrical production design. The book's sources are listed in K. Fletcher and A. Rood, *Edward Gordon Craig, a Bibliography.*

202. **Foulkes, Richard, ed.** *Shakespeare and the Victorian Stage.* Cambridge: Cambridge Univ. Press,1986.

This anthology includes such scholars as Ralph Berry, W. Moelwyn Merchant, and Simon Williams, who show how Shakespeare was refracted through Victorian culture and staging. For example, in one of the essays in Part I on the stage as picture frame, the editor shows that the "picture-framed" style of designs for Charles Kean's production of *Richard II* borrows from Pre-Raphaelite painting. Part II deals primarily with the careers of Henry Irving and Ellen Terry, and of some of their contemporaries. This review of actors is followed in Part III by accounts of Victorian productions' favoring of ancient history and imperial Rome in plays such as *Cymbeline* and *Antony.* Part IV demonstrates the domestication and pictorialization of Shakespeare by Victorians in general (as in Sullivan's musical settings), and Part V shows how he was treated in

Germany, France, and Italy during the same period. Part VI describes how he fared in provincial English theatres and on tours. The book clarifies the cultural contexts which led to the distinctive kinds of productions associated with Irving and Tree. The emergence of Victorian production values is traced from the 18th century by N. J. D. Hazleton, *Historical Consciousness in Nineteenth-Century Shakespearean Staging* (1987). There are also substantial references to Shakespeare's *Henry VIII* in M. R. Booth, *Victorian Spectacular Theatre 1850–1910* (1981).

203. **Hughes, Alan.** *Henry Irving: Shakespearean.* Cambridge: Cambridge Univ. Press, 1981.

After a chapter on Irving's approaches and methods, Hughes covers productions of individual plays (with illustrations). Chapters on tragedies include *Hamlet*, 1874, 1878; *Macbeth*, 1875, 1888; *Lear*, 1892; *Othello*, 1876, 1881; *Richard III*, 1877, 1896; *Romeo*, 1882; *Coriolanus*, 1901. Comedies covered are *Much Ado*, 1882, 1891; *Twelfth Night*, 1884; *Cymbeline*, 1896; *Merchant*, 1879. Comment on each production surveys theatrical context, script, contemporary criticism, performance, style, and modern comment. There are 39 illustrations, one appendix on texts and cuts, and a second on playbills, with casts of plays' first productions discussed. There is much detail about Irving's distinctive productions. A broader and more exhaustive account appears in L. H. F. Irving, *Henry Irving: The Actor and His World* (1951).

204. **MacMinn, George R.** *Theatre of the Golden Era in California.* Caldwell, Idaho: Caxton, 1941.

MacMinn details the rich and vigorous life of California theatre in the 1850s, in which Shakespeare revivals played a prominent part, often with internationally celebrated actors such as the Booths and Cushmans. He describes the theatres, repertories, production-styles, and reception of the principal performances, chiefly in San Francisco and Sacramento, but also in the Gold Rush country and the Central Valley generally. He points out that this period was formative in the development of a distinctive Northern California culture, largely based on theatres, in which Shakespeare predominated. A narrower version of this study, stressing a distinctively flamboyant Western style of performance, appears in H. W. Koon, *How Shakespeare Won the West: Plays and Performances in America's Gold Rush, 1849–1865* (1989).

205. **Mazer, Cary M.** *Shakespeare Refashioned: Elizabethan Plays on Edwardian Stages.* Ann Arbor: UMI Research Press, 1980.

Mazer begins with a review of Victorian precedents for the Edwardian period in the work of Irving and Tree, progressing to the Elizabethan revival led by Poel and the new stagecraft of Craig. He outlines the shifting compromises in Granville-Barker's synthesis of the reform movement and concludes with an account of Shakespeare as a director, which distinguishes between valid authenticity and effects which are merely incidental or expedient. There is an appendix covering Shakespearean productions in Greater London and Stratford-upon-Avon, 1890–1916. There are 30 plates of drawings, designs, and photographs, and an extensive bibliography. The book gives a thoughtful account of the shift from the age of Actor/Managers to Directors' theatre and the changes in production which resulted.

206. **Nash, George.** *Edward Gordon Craig: 1872–1966.* London: Her Majesty's Stationery Office, 1967.

This memorial collection of 63 plates (mostly from the Victoria and Albert Museum) is prefaced by an overview of Craig's artistic career. Apart from a few biographical photographs, the plates illustrate Craig's characteristic style as a designer, mostly displaying stage sets prepared for Shakespearean productions in the period 1898–1912, of *Hamlet, Lear, Macbeth, Much Ado, Merchant*, and *Romeo.* The designs establish Craig's distinctively bold, spare style, which the Preface shows to have greatly influenced many other Shakespeare productions in the 20th century.

207. **Payne, Ben Iden.** *A Life in the Wooden O: Memoirs of the Theatre.* New Haven: Yale Univ. Press: 1977.

This autobiography illustrates the effect of the movement to restore Elizabethan staging as advocated by William Poel, via the career of a leading figure in both commercial and academic theatres in Britain and America. It shows Payne becoming a leading advocate of the recovery of the original full scripts, the physical structure, and the fast pacing of Elizabethan staging, mostly at the University of Texas (Austin) and Carnegie Tech., and at the Stratford-upon-Avon Shakespeare Memorial Theatre, the Gaiety Theatre (Manchester, U.K.), and on New York's Broadway. At the Gaiety, Payne develops concepts of modern repertory theatre which such followers as Angus Bowmer realized in creating the Oregon Shakespeare Festival at Ashland. The book is uneven, but offers detailed impressions of how modern productions achieved Poel's goals in *Hamlet, Macbeth, Shrew, Much Ado, Measure,* and *Tempest.*

208. **Pearson, Hesketh.** *Beerbohm Tree: His Life and Laughter.* London: Methuen, 1956.

This illustrated biography of Tree puts his theatrical career in context, using primary sources provided by the producer's family, and the author's own observations of Tree and his work. It covers his theatre career as a whole rather than particular Shakespeare productions in detail, but it outlines Tree's theatrical ideas and experience, often in his own words. An appendix chronicles Tree's productions, and there is a list of sources. Tree is set in the theatrical context of Benson, the Irvings, Granville-Barker, etc., by H. Pearson, *The Last Actor Managers* (1950).

209. **Poel, William.** *Shakespeare in the Theatre.* London: Sidgwick and Jackson, 1913.

This book reprints Poel's essays on Shakespeare's playhouses, editors, and actors; on Mrs. Siddons as Lady Macbeth; on Shylock and Marlowe's Barabas; on *Henry VIII* and on *Troilus;* and on productions of *Merchant, Romeo,* and *Lear.* Poel stresses the need to restore Shakespeare's original scripts and production values as the key issue, using the first quarto of *Hamlet* as an illustration. He reviews various theatre projects such as the creation of a national theatre in the light of the need to recover Elizabethan theatre expertise.

210. **Shaw, Bernard.** *Shaw on Shakespeare.* Ed. Edwin Wilson. New York: E. P. Dutton, 1961.

Wilson collects all of Shaw's significant Shakespeare criticism, much of it exacting reviews of English productions of Shakespeare for *The Saturday Review* from January, 1896, to May, 1898; and other material related to performance of one kind or another. Shaw covers most performances in detail, discussing such figures as Mrs. Campbell, Cibber, Granville-Barker, Irving, Poel, Forbes-Robertson, Terry, and Tree. Shaw writes incisively from the perspective of the professional theatre, and more specifically as a rival dramatist to Shakespeare, often challenging conventional Victorian appreciation by anticipating modern feminisim and sociology about class roles.

211. **Speaight, Robert.** *William Poel and the Elizabethan Revival.* London: Heinemann, 1954.

Speaight covers the whole career of Poel in detail, with photographs, stressing Poel's concerns with Shakespeare as an actor; his lesser plays such as *Measure* and *Troilus*; the reduction or abandonment of intervals; the authentic use of music, costumes, and sets. He draws on detailed accounts of individual productions, ending with a chronology of Poel's productions and a bibliography of works by Poel and about him. This book is a lively, informative, and authentic account of the initiator of the 20th-century revolution in Shakespearean staging.

See also nos. 125, 126, 128, 129, 130, 131, 133, 134, 137, 139, 140, 141, 144, 146, 147, 152, 158, 186, 190, 193, 196, 197, 198, 199, 217, 223, 266, 269.

3. World War I to World War II: 1914–1945

212. **Agate, James.** *Brief Chronicles: A Survey of the Plays of Shakespeare and the Elizabethans in Actual Performance.* London: Jonathan Cape, 1943.

Agate collects his *Sunday Times* reviews of productions between 1923 and 1942, chiefly of Shakespeare (nineteen of comedies, sixteen of histories, forty-two of tragedies, two of plays of doubtful authorship), and including six of comedies and six of tragedies by other Elizabethan authors. The locales were in London (Old Vic, His Majesty's, Haymarket, Theatre Royal, Regent's Park, and the West End). While not scholarly, Agate often focuses on a single actor with useful specifics, using a strong personal perspective and bold judgments, mostly plausible.

213. **Cochrane, Claire.** *Shakespeare and the Birmingham Repertory Theatre 1913–1929.* London: Society for Theatre Research, 1993.

This illustrated study focuses on the stage director, Barry Jackson, and his professional context in the early 20th-century English theatre. It does not cover most productions in detail, but pays attention to the 1913 opening of *Twelfth Night* and subsequent progression from elaborately realistic productions to more sparely suggestive ones, as favored by the design of Gordon Craig. Cochrane covers many aspects of the theatre's history, including actors, directors, designers, and reception. Chapters 6 and 7, on Shakespeare in modern dress, include discussion of *All's Well* (1927) and the failed *Macbeth* (1928). The Appendix chronicles productions, with directors and designers. There is a select bibliography.

214. **Farjeon, Herbert.** *The Shakespeare Scene: Dramatic Criticism.* London: Hutchinson, no date.

These 108 reviews from magazines and newspapers cover Shakespeare performances in London from 1918 to 1944, grouped as Comedies, Histories, and Tragedies, often providing notes about several productions under the title of each play, so that one can compare, for example, Casson's 1926 *Henry VIII* (with Sybil Thorndike) to Guthrie's in 1933 (with Flora Robson and Charles Laughton), followed by the Open Air Theatre's version in Regent's Park in 1936. The accounts are subjective and casual, neither analytic nor profound, but they provide considerable detail about the performances, such as the account of the fiasco of the 1925 Old Vic *Much Ado.*

215. **Guthrie, Tyrone.** *A Life in the Theatre.* London: Hamish Hamilton, 1961.

Guthrie writes about his personal life including his theatrical career, with frequent allusions to Shakespeare, to his own productions of Shakespeare's plays (particularly at the Old Vic, Stratford-upon-Avon, and Stratford-Ontario), and to those of his contemporaries and predecessors. Some of Guthrie's achievements come later than this publication, but this material is relevant to the understanding of his whole career as an innovator in Shakespearean production.

216. **Harwood, Ronald.** *Sir Donald Wolfit C.B.E.: His Life and Work in the Unfashionable Theatre.* London: Secker and Warburg, 1971.

This is a detailed biography of a latter-day actor/manager in the traditional vein, who played principal roles at the Old Vic, Stratford-upon-Avon, Hammersmith, and who also toured across North America and Africa during World War II. The book describes many of his roles, including an effective Petruchio and Benedick; a distinctive Othello, who fails to consummate his marriage; and a psychologically evolving Lear. Harwood indicates that Wolfit remained controversial, partly because of his company's limited sets and costumes. He also shows that Wolfitt sustained a heroic production schedule during the war, as reflected in appendices listing his roles and the actors who worked with him.

217. **Knight, G. Wilson.** *Principles of Shakespeare Production.* London: Faber and Faber, 1936. Repr.: Harmondsworth: Penguin, 1949. Revised as *Shakespearean Production: with Especial Reference to the Tragedies.* London: Faber and Faber, 1964.

This book derives from a lifetime of observation and of experience in Shakespearean production. It includes substantial defence of Beerbohm Tree based on Knight's first-hand observation, and it reviews other directors' stage productions. It also covers Knight's own concerns as a director. The book refracts performance through Knight's assumptions about essential meanings of the plays, illustrating the correlation of critical interpretation with actual performance. The work is discontinuous and discursive, but it comments helpfully on many 20th-century theatrical interpreters of Shakespeare.

218. **Miller, John.** *Ralph Richardson: The Authorized Biography.* London: Sidgwick and Jackson, 1990.

This chronological survey includes references to Richardson's many Shakespearean performances, discussing their social and artistic context, their professional character, and their reception. Appendices cover Richardson's parts, films, television and radio appearances, and a bibliography. The comprehensiveness permits less detailed coverage.

219. **Olivier, Laurence.** *On Acting.* New York: Simon and Schuster, 1986.

This subjective account provides personal data, historical detail, and professional insights relating to all of Olivier's major Shakespeare roles and productions, both on stage and in film, such as *Hamlet, Richard III*, and *Othello*. While anecdotal and hardly scholarly, the book provides authentic, detailed information about Olivier's career, theatrical motivations, and artistic methods.

220. **Sprague, Arthur Colby, and J. C. Trewin.** *Shakespeare's Plays Today: Some Customs and Conventions of the Stage.* Columbia: Univ. of South Carolina Press, 1970.

This book reviews the evolution of theatrical business in staging Shakespeare chiefly in the first two-thirds of the 20th century. Chapter headings include "Stage Business"; "Cutting the Text"; "Additions to the Text"; "Speaking the Lines"; "Sights and Sounds"; "People of the Plays"; and "Stages and Staging." While discursive and selective, it has many exact observations of modern developments, such as the shift from a mature, lady-like Olivia to a girlish romantic; the recovery of the once-cut masque in *Cymbeline;* the development of costuming conventions, as with many modern barefoot Audreys, while most Falstaffs now usually appear in large boots; the frequent cutting of Fortinbras and the Ambassadors, contrasting with the common addition of Mistress Shore to the cast of *Richard III* and of Kate Keepdown to that of *Measure*. The book is casual and subjective but lively and alert to stage minutiae.

221. **Styan John L.** *The Shakespeare Revolution: Criticism and Performance in the Twentieth Century.* Cambridge: Cambridge Univ. Press, 1977.

Styan reviews modern changes in Shakespeare production since Victorian times, led by Poel, and their increasing effect through stage-centered literary criticism. Styan stresses the innovative roles of Barker, Playfair, and Jackson, with special chapters on Guthrie's use of the open stage and Peter Brook's rejection of theatre illusion. Styan notes the correlation of such techniques with the recovery of Elizabethan staging, with its stress on non-realistic effects of allegory and symbolism.

222. **Trewin, John Courtney.** *Benson and the Bensonians.* London: Barnes and Rockliff, 1960.

Trewin covers Shakespeare-director Frank Benson's career from his early tours with William Poel, including his long association with the development of Stratford-upon-Avon's Memorial Theatre, and with the London Lyceum, as well as his company's major tours in the U.K. and overseas. Benson's association with Ellen Terry is described, and his sequence of early Shakespearean films. The book concludes with a useful note on its sources.

223. **Trewin, John Courtney.** *Going to Shakespeare.* London: Allen and Unwin, 1978.

Trewin consolidates his reviews of productions of every Shakespeare play but *Kinsmen*, comparing and contrasting some 1,500 performances in various U.K. locations. He stresses performance values, with useful asides on such topics as Phelps' revival of *Pericles* (1854), and Edith Evans speaking Rosalind's Epilogue in "a quick blaze of Millamantine sophistication" as "a Restoration belle" (145). The reprinted items are brief and often best on lesser plays, as in his remarks on Isabella's final silence in *Measure* or the seasons evoked in *Merry Wives*. The author is more casual and anecdotal in his earlier book, *Shakespeare on the English Stage, 1900–1964* (1964).

224. **Vallillo, Stephen M.** "The Shakespeare Productions of the Federal Theatre Project." *Theatre History Studies* 3 (1983): 28–53.

This illustrated overview of Federal-Government-sponsored Shakespeare in the 1930s notes thirty-one productions. It quotes contemporary reviews, showing that these productions had considerable success through shared production values, as they often stressed current political issues such as dictatorship and were given immediacy by modern dress and use of minority actors, mostly African-American. With simplified sets and bold effects, these productions often match the success of the best-known one: Orson Welles' *Macbeth*.

See also nos. 126, 130, 131, 133, 134, 137, 139, 146, 147, 148, 149, 186, 187, 189, 190, 192, 194, 195, 197, 198, 199, 226, 230, 245, 249, 255, 267.

4. The Contemporary Period 1945–1998

225. **Addenbrooke, David.** *The Royal Shakespeare Company: The Peter Hall Years.* London: William Kimber, 1974.

This book provides an illustrated overview of all aspects of the Royal Shakespeare Company as led by Peter Hall 1960–74, a key phase at the Stratford-upon-Avon theatre. Part I covers development of the R.S.C. Part II prints personal interviews with Peggy Ashcroft, John Barton, John Bury, Peter Hall, Clifford Williams, and David Brierly. Part III has appendices on administration, audiences, contracts, productions, staff, policy, and awards. The book fully explains company operations and productions, such as the staging of the English history plays as *The Wars of the Roses*, and its film version. There is less detail about individual performances.

226. **Babula, William.** *Shakespeare in Production, 1935–1978: A Selective Catalogue.* New York: Garland, 1981.

This bibliography selects unusual productions in the United States, Canada, and England, leaving out excellent but straightforward ones. Entries note each production's location, director, date, and summaries of selected reviews from many sources. There is an index of theatres, companies, and festivals, plus another of directors. Many major productions are noted briefly.

227. **Berry, Ralph.** *Changing Styles in Shakespeare.* London: Allen and Unwin, 1981.

Berry describes the congruent changes in stage interpretations of Shakespeare in the post-war period, finding a shift towards a plainer, harsher, more intellectual, anti-romantic strain, based on a sense of the script's social relevance to bad modern conditions. He makes his point by alluding to recent productions of *Coriolanus* (with the hero no longer noble), *Troilus* (used brutally against the political establishment), *Henry V* (no longer accepted as a patriotic play), *Twelfth Night* (seen as dark comedy), and *Hamlet* (de-romanticized). He suggests that Kott's Brechtian view of *Lear* will triumph as audiences get to know the film versions by Brook and Kozintsev.

228. **Berry, Ralph, ed.** *On Directing Shakespeare: Interviews with Contemporary Directors.* London: Hamish Hamilton, 1989.

Berry interviews prominent directors of the eighties. Jonathan Miller discusses the fashion for modern referentiality as in the postcolonial readings of *Tempest*. Konrad Swinarski explains the contemporary political implications of his productions of *All's Well* and of *Dream* (in which Quince's missing Epilogue is the clue to the play's subversion of authority). Trevor Nunn explains his vision of the R.S.C. repertory, and Peter Brook his activities in France and the U.S.A. The eclecticism favored by Robin Phillips and the populism of Michael Bogdanov's *Henry VI* contrast with the rigorous Renaissance periodization of Peter Hall. Bill Alexander explains his didactic concept of *Richard III* as played by Antony Sher, and Giorgio Strehler, Michael Kahn, and Declan Donnellan (of Cheek by Jowl) outline their production philosophies. While no production is fully covered, these interviews provide personal statements by directors and their peers applicable to noted modern productions.

229. **Bogdanov, Michael, and Michael Pennington.** *The English Shakespeare Company: The Story of "The Wars of the Roses" 1986–1989.* London: Nick Hern, 1990.

The book describes the origins, character, and history of the global tour by the English Shakespeare Company's production of Shakespeare's English history plays under the title of *The Wars of the Roses*. The book describes the challenges and achievements of a touring repertory company, not limited to artistic issues but covering the less picturesque details of finance, administration, casting, and logistics. It gives a realistic expression of the texture of postmodern theatrical life in which traditional solutions to production problems and conventional artistic expectations in performance are rejected in favor of radical shifts of set design, costuming, and acting style.

230. **Bowmer, Angus L.** *As I remember, Adam: An Autobiography of a Festival.* Ashland: Oregon Shakespeare Festival Association, 1975.

This autobiography describes the evolution from 1934 of one the leading Shakespeare festivals in the U.S.A. It identifies the influence of Iden Payne on the author's determination to shift the teaching of Shakespeare from pedantic to production values, and traces the vicissitudes in funding, building, and artistic achievement down to the establishment of the current exemplary modern theatrical complex. Incidentally, the narrative provides many aperçus of modern theatrical activities world-wide as they relate to Shakespeare, such as reviews of the young Olivier at the Old Vic, playing Hamlet and Sir Toby Belch. This history provides an archetype of the pattern found more recently in the creation of over a hundred similar institutions throughout the U.S.A.

231. **Brockbank, Philip, ed.** *Players of Shakespeare: Essays in Shakespeare Performance by Twelve Players with the Royal Shakespeare Company.* Cambridge: Cambridge Univ. Press, 1985.

Brockbank offers a collection of modern performers' views of their roles in short essays: Patrick Stewart (Shylock, 1979), Sinéad Cusack (Portia, 1981), Donald Sinden (Malvolio, 1969), John Bowe (Orlando, 1980), Brenda Bruce (Juliet's Nurse, 1980), Geoffrey Hutchings (Lavatch in *All's Well,* 1981), Tony Church (Polonius, 1965), Michael Pennington (Hamlet, 1980), Richard Pasco (Timon, 1980), Roger Rees (Posthumus in *Cymbeline,* 1979), Gemma Jones (Hermione in *Winter's Tale,* 1981), and David Suchet (Caliban in *Tempest,* 1978). This volume stresses the subjective approach of the actors to their own roles rather than overviews of whole productions, but incidentally it often provides a broader background. The volume was reprinted in 1988 as the first of a series of such anthologies, including *Players of Shakespeare II* and *III,* both subtitled: *Further Essays in Shakespeare Performance by Players with the Royal Shakespeare Company,* ed. R. Jackson and R. Smallwood (1988; 1993).

232. **Brook, Peter.** *The Empty Space.* London: McGibbon and Kee, 1968; Harmondsworth: Penguin, 1972.

Brook's four lectures define types of production. (1) Deadly

Theatre, he says, is marked by antiquarian, low intensity, traditional performance. (2) Holy Theatre he defines as highly contemporary, with ritualistic happenings. (3) Rough Theatre for him involves popular, lively, inexpensive production in the style of Poel, Brecht, and Craig, with a Marxist twist. (4) Immediate Theatre rejects use of designers and rehearsals, according to Brook, who wishes actors to respond directly to audiences, using a bold acting style. The book outlines the credo of a radical, modern director of major Shakespeare productions, to which it largely applies: Brook says Shakespearean productions usually match types (2) and (3) if presented in authentic Elizabethan terms. A broader coverage appears in P. Brook, *The Shifting Point: Theatre, Film, Opera, 1947–1987* (1987). See also D. Williams, ed., *Peter Brook: A Theatrical Casebook* (1987).

233. **Brown, Ivor, and Anthony Quayle.** *Shakespeare Memorial Theatre 1948–1950: A Photographic Record.* London: Reinhardt and Evans, 1951.

This anthology of photographs is preceded by two essays by the listed authors, Brown's covering the history of the Stratford Memorial Theatre, and the other essay the experience of Quayle as director there, followed by eighty pages of production shots by the theatre photographer, Angus McBean, whose lifetime collection of theatre photography is now at Harvard University. The period recorded marks the rise of the Stratford theatre towards its current international distinction. The productions involve twenty-one plays, including such noted productions as the *Henry VIII* of Tyrone Guthrie; the frequently revived *Much Ado* of John Gielgud (with Peggy Ashcroft) and his *Lear* of 1950; and various performances by Godfrey Tearle (Othello, Macbeth), Robert Helpman (King John, Shylock, Hamlet), Paul Scofield (Hamlet, Roderigo), Harry Andrews (Don Pedro, Wolsey), and numerous roles by Antony Quayle himself. These photographs provide valuable records of costumes, sets, and blocking, representative of Shakespeare production during this period.

234. **Brown, John Russell.** *Free Shakespeare.* London: Heinemann, 1974.

These published lectures argue for ways of performing Shakespeare, nearer to Elizabethan practice, and suited to the limitations of amateur and student productions. Brown attacks current professional styles of production such as those of Peter Brook. He dislikes stress on directors', designers', and actors' "choices" as in Brook's notorious *Dream*. He rejects the use of star performers and over-rehearsal of scripts, and he favors impromptus; non-pictorial, open, thrust stages; and interpretations discovered in concert with the audience. He questions directors' traditional authority by reporting experiments with actors lacking such formal direction, and he discusses these experiments' outcomes. Brown provides a late version of Poel's views about reducing modern over-elaborate productions to Elizabethan spareness.

235. **Brown, John Russell.** *Shakespeare's Plays in Performance.* London: Edward Arnold, 1966. Revised, New York: Applause Books, 1993.

In Part I, Brown explores the relation of actors to texts in terms of verbal drama, acting, gestures and business, subtext, roles, and laughter, with detailed references to historical performances. Part II considers Action and the Stage, using *Richard II* for narrative and focus, and *Hamlet* for setting, grouping, movement, and tempo. Part III considers the play and its audience. Part IV looks at such sixties productions as Zeffirelli's *Romeo* at the Old Vic (1960–62), with a chapter on *Twelfth Night*. An Appendix on "Theatre Research and the Criticism of Shakespeare and His Contemporaries" argues for the importance of performance studies. There are also 21 illustrations of Shakespearean sets and actors. The book contains illuminating comments on many other significant modern productions such as the Barton-Hall cycle of the English history plays at the R.S.C. (1964).

236. **Bulman, James C., ed.** *Shakespeare, Theory, and Performance.* London: Routledge, 1996.

This anthology of essays by teachers of English outlines current critical approaches to study of Shakespeare in performance. James Bulman questions the meaningfulness of citing a definable author called Shakespeare. W. B. Worthen argues that contemporaneity rules in any presentation of Shakespeare's scripts, and that there is no valid stable Shakespearean characterization. Anthony Dawson develops Foucault's stress on the actor's bodily presence as the determining factor in performance. Juliet Dusinberre discusses the gender-challenging effect of the boy actor originally playing Cleopatra in contrast to the role's impact when played by an actress. Barbara Hodgdon uses Robert Lepage's 1992 *Dream* to re-site Shakespeare in a modern multi-cultural world. Richard Knowles, one of the two drama teachers involved, discusses how vocal divergences and voice training bear on Shakespeare performance. Denis Salter reviews problems in relating to Shakespeare for actors in post-colonialist societies. Dennis Kennedy discusses the aesthetic advantages of performing Shakespeare in foreign language translations. Cary Mazer reviews author-recognition in stage-focused Shakespeare scholarship, as illustrated by Alan Dessen. He relates this historical role of the dramatist to the modern, thematically unified R.S.C. staging of Shakespeare in the sixties. Laurie Osborne discusses performance editions. Douglas Lanier relates Greenaway's *Prospero's Books* to the text of *Tempest*. The anthology offers a cross-section of the approaches by scholars and teachers teaching Shakespeare through performance.

237. **Cooper, Roberta Krensky.** *The American Shakespeare Theatre: Stratford, 1955–1985.* Washington, D.C.: Folger Shakespeare Library/Associated Univ. Presses, 1986.

Previously director of planning at the Stratford Festival, the author describes its first thirty years, covering financial, administrative, and artistic concerns, with details of all productions and their reception. She reviews the work of John Houseman and Michael Kahn as Artistic Directors, and such noted seasons as Christopher Plummer's (1981), in which he played Iago to James Earl Jones' Othello and doubled the role of Chorus with that of Henry V (seen as a more mature king reviewing his own youthful career). The study illustrates the issues raised in the creation of a Shakespeare repertory theatre in North America: problems of stage design, artistic policy, financial base, recruitment of directors, and a loyal audience.

238. **Coursen, Herbert.** *Reading Shakespeare on Stage.* Newark: Univ. of Delaware Press, 1995.

Coursen begins with discussion of television's impact on reactions to live performances and how these are affected by scripting and performance spaces. He then reviews productions, 1987–93, considering story line, performance space, delivery, design, genre, and reception. Productions discussed include Peter Hall's *Antony, Merchant,* and *All's Well;* the *Lear*s of David Hare, Deborah Warner, Kenneth Branagh, Max Stafford-Clark, and Nicolas Hytner; Warner's *Titus,* Terry Hands' *Caesar;* Bill Alexander's *Twelfth Night, Shrew,* and *Cymbeline;* Adrian Noble's *Plantagenets* (based on Shakespeare's histories), *Winter's Tale,* and *Hamlet;* Robert Lepage's *Dream;* Richard Eyre's *Richard III;* the *Hamlet*s of Ron Daniels and Michael Kahn; Michael Bogdanov's *Macbeth;* Michael Langham's *Measure;* Robert Egan's *Richard II;* and Maria Aikens' *As You Like It.*

239. **Coursen, Herbert.** *Shakespearean Performance as Interpretation.* Newark: Univ. of Delaware Press, 1992.

Coursen considers the issues raised by the performance of a particular script in a specific place as registered by the subjective viewpoint of a modern spectator. He finds feminism the best formulation from which to derive a modern point of view about performance and accordingly devotes his opening chapters to Kate (in *Shrew*); Hermia; and Ophelia. He then broadens to Jacobi's reading of Hamlet and the Players; to two chapters on *Lear,* one focused on Edmund, and the other on Lear and Cordelia. Another chapter reviews the treatment of the history plays by directors such as Howell, Hands, Barton, and Branagh. Finally, in a chapter on television versions, he censures the Papp/Antoon television video of *Much Ado* for its anachronism, and juxtaposes the BBC series' *Antony* with Trevor Nunn's 1975 version. Each production is treated as a unique critical experience.

240. **Crowl, Samuel.** *Shakespeare Observed: Studies in Performance on Stage and Screen.* Athens: Ohio Univ. Press, 1992.

Crowl shows how successive productions interact, such as the influence of Roman Polanski's film of *Macbeth* (1971) on Adrian Noble's 1984 stage production of the play. In similar terms he examines the interrelationships of films and plays produced by other major figures such as Orson Welles, Peter Hall, Derek Jarman, Michael Bogdanov, and Kenneth Branagh. He uses material about their careers and personalities to confirm his interpretations of their works.

241. **David, Richard,** *Shakespeare in the Theatre.* Cambridge: Cambridge Univ. Press, 1978.

David discusses performance issues based on detailed studies of key moments in major English productions of the 1970s, often noting their evolution in extended runs. His account of directorial roles stresses Trevor Nunn's sequence of Roman histories, *Antony, Coriolanus, Caesar,* and *Titus* (1972–73); John Barton's *Richard II* (1972) and *John* (1974); and Terry Hands' versions of *Henry IV* (1975). Davis covers topicality in Brook's use of Kott in his *Dream* (1970); and racial implications in John Barton's Indian setting of *Much Ado* with Sinden and Dench (1976), and in various productions of *Othello*. The book reviews new priorities in recent productions.

242. **Dollimore, Jonathan, and Alan Sinfield, eds.** *Political Shakespeare: New Essays in Cultural Materialism.* Manchester: Manchester Univ. Press, 1985. Revised, 1994.

This anthology illustrates the work of recent Shakespeare critics influenced by Raymond Williams. They review performance values in modern Shakespeare productions such as the R.S.C.'s, taking particular note of Peter Hall's use of Jan Kott in *The Wars of the Roses* (1964). Sinfield also explores Peter Brook's modernist distrust of historical relevance. Sharing Foucault's rejection of the unifying author, Sinfield describes how modern interpretations of "Shakespeare" use him as a political icon. Graham Holderness applies a similar critique to film and television versions. Margaret Heinemann defines Brecht's redirection of Shakespeare performance in East Germany. The anthology includes many bold judgments, as in Sinfield's attack on the glamorization of productions at the R.S.C. in the '80s.

243. **Engle, Ron, Felicia Hardison Londré, and Daniel J. Watermeier, eds.** *Shakespeare Companies and Festivals: An International Guide.* Westport, Conn.: Greenwood Press, 1995.

This fully-annotated list provides exhaustive coverage of over 150 significant Shakespeare repertory groups, principally covering the U.S.A. state by state, but also with entries for Australia, Austria, Canada, China, France, Germany, Great Britain, Japan, New Zealand, South Africa, Spain, and Switzerland. Entries note company histories with staffing and budget; physical facilities and performance site; demographics and community; and approach to Shakespeare. Most entries also have one review of a first performance. Headnotes cover a company's origins, with its official name, address, phone number, ticket prices, season dates, and Equity status, followed by a chronological summary of Shakespeare plays produced, and reference sources.

244. **Gay, Penny.** *As She Likes It: Shakespeare's Unruly Women.* London: Routledge, 1994.

Gay uses a feminist approach in describing and analyzing many productions of five Shakespearean comedies frequently performed since World War II at Stratford-upon-Avon. These are illustrated by eighteen photographs. She sets the production details of numerous performances and their reception in a context of traditional patriarchy and archaic gender roles. However, she sees *Twelfth Night* as evolving currently from a romantic comedy into a problematic study of fluctuating identities and genders. She finds *As You Like It* to be "a powerful fantasy of liberation"(48) from "an extremely unpleasant contemporary real world" (85), while admitting the primacy of Vanessa Redgrave's upbeat Rosalind (1961). For Gay, *Shrew* can be accepted nowadays only in Marowitz' "horrific reworking," with its "physical torture and madness of Kate" (104; see no. 258). Gay finds that *Measure* better accommodates contemporary "growing awareness of sexual harassment" (121). The realism of *Much Ado* is welcome to her as this play can now display "the powerful coercion of our social system" (143), a view anticipated by the Gielgud production (1949) with Peggy Ashcroft. She considers Nunn and Barton to be forward-looking in their less hopeful readings of their scripts; but she judges the latter's Indian Raj setting of

Much Ado to be offensive to multi-culturalism. The book illustrates the relevance of feminist interpretations to performance while evoking the exact character of many noted modern productions.

245. **Gielgud, John, with John Miller.** *Acting Shakespeare.* London: Sidgwick and Jackson, 1991; New York: Scribner's, 1992.

This autobiographical account, with numerous photographs, presents a subjective perspective of the many significant Shakespeare stage productions (Granville-Barker's *Lear*, and the often revived *Much Ado* with Peggy Ashcroft, among others) and films (such as Greenaway's *Prospero's Books*, and Welles' *Chimes at Midnight*) in which Gielgud has acted (as with the Old Vic *Hamlet*) or directed. He gives a subjective account of the concerns, procedures, and outcomes, with insights into the work of such colleagues and friends as Ralph Richardson. Gielgud shows how his personal and sentimental appreciation of the texts affected his performance choices. There is a list of Shakespeare productions which Gielgud has directed. This is not a rigorously-argued academic study, but it does explain informally how actors' personal approaches affect their professional concerns. Though it is not so focused, there is also much reference to Gielgud's Shakespeare roles in his revised autobiography, J. Gielgud, *An Actor and His Time* (1989).

246. **Greenwald, Michael L.** *Directions by Indirections: John Barton of the Royal Shakespeare Company.* Newark: Univ. of Delaware Press: 1985.

Greenwald covers John Barton's career at the R.S.C., 1960–1984, after briefly reviewing influences during his study at Cambridge University. The coverage is play by play of more than thirty productions (mostly Shakespeare) with attention given to the rehearsal process as well as the finished production and the critical responses to it. Stress is laid on the scholarly and critical interpretations Barton brought to each play, and on the directness and simplicity of style which he derived from his interest in Poel's theories about Elizabethan production. The book notes Barton's Chekhovian restraint in the acting style he prefers, and his often bold adaptation of the scripts is treated critically. The book is thorough in coverage of an influential British theatrical career, showing how it helped to set the distinctively sociological R.S.C. production style for many years, beginning with the 1963–64 productions of *The Wars of the Roses*.

247. **Halio, Jay.** *Understanding Shakespeare's Plays in Performance.* Manchester: Manchester Univ. Press, 1988.

In reviewing modern audiences' experience of Shakespeare in the theatre and cinema, Halio provides an overview of the late 20th-century productions by such directors as Barton, Bogdanov, Brook, Guthrie, Hall, Kahn, Kozintsev, Miller, Noble, and Welles. He includes references to less obvious productions by regional companies. Chapters cover set design, characterization, subtext, language, stage business, and concept. The book is brief but precise enough in its references to significant productions to give a useful summation of current practices in staging Shakespeare in the U.K. and the U.S.A.

248. **Hall, Peter.** *Diaries: The Story of a Dramatic Battle.* New York: Harper and Rowe, 1984.

Hall narrates his experiences as Director in inaugurating the National Theatre in London, 1972–1980. While Shakespeare productions are only part of this operation, his diary communicates the artistic, economic, administrative, and political issues affecting theatrical life in the seventies. The procedures and problems in staging major productions are described and relate to such performances of Shakespeare as the National Theatre *Hamlet* (1975) and *Macbeth* (1978), both featuring Albert Finney. There are comments on other modern Shakespearean productions, mostly by the Royal Shakespeare Company, and discussions of Shakespearean actors such as Peggy Ashcroft, John Gielgud, Laurence Olivier, Ralph Richardson, and Paul Scofield. Hall reviews the directorial skills of Peter Brook and Trevor Nunn, and his own artistic values and expertise. Hall evaluates various theatres and compares Shakespeare with Jonson and Marlowe. The book aids understanding of the professional context of modern Shakespeare production.

249. **Hildy, Franklin J.** *Shakespeare at the Maddermarket: Nugent Monk and the Norwich Players.* Ann Arbor, Mich.: U.M.I. Research Press, 1986.

Hildy chronicles the Maddermarket Theatre in Norwich, opened in 1921, and directed by Nugent Monk. He shows Monk rejecting the convention of the proscenium arch in pursuing the concern of William Poel to re-establish Elizabethan principles of performance, which led the way for the 20th-century Little Theatre Movement in Britain and America, and to a more authentic production of Renaissance plays. Detailed accounts of the productions and their influence demonstrate Monk's contribution to the careers and values of directors such as Harcourt Williams and Tyrone Guthrie. As the first director to complete production of all of Shakespeare's plays, Monk also fostered interest in neglected scripts. The book is illustrated and has detailed tables of Monk's productions, 1900–58, and a bibliography. Hildy shows the provincial repertory theatre's contribution to the national history of Shakespeare production.

250. **Holderness, Graham, ed.** *The Shakespeare Myth.* Manchester: Manchester Univ. Press, 1988.

This anthology provides a detailed critique by Cultural Materialists of Shakespeare as presented in media, popular culture, and performance. The editor questions Sam Wanamaker on his rebuilding of the Globe Theatre, which is also reviewed later in the book by John Drakakis. Derek Longhurst sees a shift from cultural hero to parodist as Shakespeare's modern role in popular culture. Ann Thompson's feminist readings of Shakespeare lead to an interview with Michael Bogdanov about his R.S.C. production of *Shrew* in 1978 and his other interpretations. Christopher McCullough writes of current theatre practices derived from F. R. Leavis by Peter Hall and Trevor Nunn, taking a Brechtian view of Cambridge radicalism. Interviewing Terry Hands, McCullough discusses the R.S.C.'s relationship to the political establishment. Alan Sinfield reviews the challenges raised in Shakespeare rewritings by Stoppard and Bond. David Hornbrook defines Shakespeare's role in education, and John Hodgson shows how to enhance Shakespeare by more performance in schools, as demonstrated by Michael Croft. Holderness questions the assumptions of the BBC TV series, via interviews with its literary advisor, John Wilders, and one of its directors, Jonathan Miller.

The book scrutinizes skeptically most major institutions presenting Shakespeare.

251. **Holland, Peter.** *English Shakespeares.* Cambridge: Cambridge Univ. Press, 1997.

Holland considers factors affecting modern productions of Shakespeare, such as the character of the theatres, directors, designers, actors, and regional setting. He surveys productions from 1989 to 1995 by the Royal Shakespeare Company, the National Theatre, Cheek by Jowl, Northern Broadsides, and the English Shakespeare Company. A final chapter considers productions outside England. An experienced reviewer, Holland provides precise notes on significant productions, such as the Eyre/McKellen production of *Richard III* (1990; turned into a film, 1996). See also Peter Holland, "Stratford Stages: Two Interviews," *Shakespeare Survey* 27 (1994): 117–26, recording an interview with Michael Reardon and Tim Furby about their designs for the Swan Theatre and the new Other Place, and their alterations to the main theatre at Stratford-upon-Avon. He then interviews Sam Mendes, the director of *Troilus* (1990) in the Swan; of *Richard III* (1992) staged first in the Swan, then in the Tokyo Globe, and last in the Other Place; and of *Tempest* in the main theatre.

252. **Hunt, Albert, and Geoffrey Reeves.** *Peter Brook.* Cambridge: Cambridge Univ. Press: 1995.

This overview of Peter Brook's career in the theatre devotes several chapters to his Shakespearean productions. Chapter 3 deals with *Lear* (Stratford-upon-Avon, 1962). Chapter 9 dicusses *Tempest* (Stratford, 1957). Chapter 10 describes the genesis at Stratford of Brook's noted white box version of *Dream*. In Chapter 15 the productions shift to Paris for *Timon* (1974) and *Measure* (1978); then back to Stratford for *Antony* (1979). The concluding Chapter 19 deals with a Parisian version of *Tempest* (1990). The book establishes the director's artistic ethos in each production, its sources, personal development, application to the specific text, and outcome. The book opens with a chronology of Brook's productions and ends with a bibliography of books, interviews, and articles involving Brook.

253. **King, Christine, and Brenda Coven.** *Joseph Papp and the New York Shakespeare Festival: An Annotated Bibliography.* New York: Garland, 1988.

This selective bibliography begins with a life and career chronology of Joseph Papp and the New York Shakespeare Festival, with a list of Papp's own publications. Next come entries for books and magazine articles about Papp, listed by author. Then follows a chronological list of newspaper references, citing only play reviews selected from the *New York Times.* Many entries concern the financial, administrative, and political aspects of Papp's career. However, the volume provides a chronology of the Festival's major productions, including many plays by Shakespeare; a list of major productions by title; and author and subject indexes. The bibliography outlines the facts of Papp's work in the theatre, but aesthetic concerns are underplayed (e.g., the Index notes only a reply to the *Times* review, Item 36).

254. **Kott, Jan.** *Shakespeare Our Contemporary.* Trans. Boleslaw Taborski. Garden City, New York: Doubleday, 1964.

This Polish director argues for assimilation of Shakespeare to 20th-century views, reflecting the doctrines of Freud, Marx, and their successors, as seen in the theater. He rejects traditional, picturesque, or romantic productions. His harsh revisionist readings in the spirit of Brecht cover the major tragedies, *Dream, Tempest,* and *As You Like It.* Kott's book has influenced the updating of Shakespeare's plays, as in Peter Brook's circus version of *Dream,* and his film of *Lear* which followed Kott's comparison of it with Beckett's *Endgame.*

255. **Leaming, Barbara.** *Orson Welles.* New York: Viking, 1985.

This detailed biography of Welles places his Shakespeare productions in full context, giving substantial coverage to both stage and screen versions, including his work for the Federal Theatre Project. It reviews the personal, professional, financial, and aesthetic aspects of the creation of these works. It also locates Welles clearly in the theatre and cinematic milieux of his time, using the maximum range of available sources, as recorded in the footnotes. While not devoted only to his achievement with Shakespeare, the text assists in defining it by voluminous circumstantial detail.

256. **Leiter, Samuel L., ed.** *Shakespeare Around the Globe: A Guide to Notable Postwar Revivals.* New York: Greenwood, 1986.

This encyclopedia covers the plays in alphabetical order. Five essayists (Langdon Brown, Felicia Londré, Tice Miller, Michael Mullin, and Daniel Watermeier) deal with groups of plays, aided by invited reviewers of individual productions (1945–85). Each entry includes a preliminary essay, then reviews of recent productions with the director, major cast, locations, and dates. These entries may cover 22 reviews of a play like *Tempest* (with reviews of both Strehler productions, 1948, 1978), or only a single review of *Kinsmen* (despite other recent productions). There is much production data in the reviews; and there are useful indexes, including ones covering revivals, artists, and critics not reviewed in this volume.

257. **Londré, Felicia H.** "Confronting Shakespeare's 'Political Incorrectness' in Production: Contemporary American Audiences and the New 'Problem Plays.'" In *Staging Difference: Cultural Pluralism in American Theatre and Drama*, ed. Marc Maufort, 85–95. New York: Peter Lang, 1995.

Londré examines the problems raised for directors of *Othello, Shrew,* and *Merchant* by modern, politicized attitudes towards race and gender, and she describes the creative options unveiled by directors' solutions to such problems.

258. **Marowitz, Charles.** *Recycling Shakespeare.* New York: Applause, 1991.

Marowitz represents the post-modernist revolution dominating the theatre of the 1990s. Following Stanislavsky, Brecht, Artaud, and Jan Kott (whose interview by Marowitz is included), Marowitz argues for the total artistic and intellectual superiority of the director over the dramatist (and everyone else), if texts are to be assimilated by modern audiences. Radical dismemberment of Shakespearean scripts is advocated, based on what Marowitz asserts is their author's inferior understanding of theatre compared to that of current directors (as proved by the views of Shakespeare's characters, such as Hamlet). The book rejects "academic" concerns, and those of John Russell Brown, Peter Hall, John Barton, Kenneth Branagh, and other contemporary scholars, critics, and directors. Radically restructured stage interpretations matching Marowitz's revisionist views are offered of *Shrew, Measure, Hamlet, Macbeth,* and *Caesar* (exemplified in the book by a "recycled" script of *Caesar* reassigning many lines to different characters). The book explains why many modern productions ignore the author, his scripts, and original conditions of production: no congruity with the past is possible. Some texts of Marowitz adaptations are available in *The Marowitz Shakespeare* (1978).

259. **Miller, Jonathan.** *Subsequent Performances.* London: Faber and Faber, 1986.

Miller begins with a theoretical defense of modern directors' domination of the theatre and performance as inevitable in the recreation of classic plays. He then moves on to consider his own productions in the context of modern directorial theatre, including extensive discussion of *Shrew, Dream, Merchant, Troilus, Hamlet, Lear, Othello,* and *Tempest.* He discusses differences between his live and filmed productions. The book is most effective in its discussion of individual productions.

260. **Price, Joseph G., ed.** *The Triple Bond: Plays, Mainly Shakespearean, in Performance.* University Park: Pennsylvania State Univ. Press, 1975.

Part I of this collection, about interpretation, includes Stanley Wells on critics and theatre professionals; M. St. Claire Byrne on intention and realization in *Henry VIII*; and Muriel Bradbrook on audiences. In Part II, on audiences, Clifford Leach writes on song as ironic chorus; Anne Barton on kingly disguise in *Henry V*; Frances Shirley on oaths; and J. C. Trewin about off-stage characters. Part III covers performance, with Jane Williamson on Duke Vincentio and Isabella (*Measure*); Lois Potter on *Duchess of Malfi*; Jeanne Newlin on Kemble and *Troilus;* and Robert Ball on the 1929 Pickford-Fairbanks *Shrew.* Part IV deals with theatres, with Nevill Coghill on *Macbeth* at the Globe; Alan Downer on *Antony* as first performed; Rudolph Stamm on Lavinia's muteness in *Titus;* and

Sybil Rosenfeld on the designer Herbert Herkomer. There is a bibliography of Arthur Sprague's publications, the model for the book's stress on interpretation by performance.

261. **Prosser, William LLewellyn.** *American Directorial Approaches to Shakespeare, 1960–1976.* Ann Arbor: Xerox Univ. Microfilms, 1977.

This City University of New York Ph.D. thesis covers eight directors: Stuart Vaughan, Joseph Papp, Gerald Freedman, Allen Fletcher, William Ball, Edward Cole, Michael Kahn, and Nagle Jackson. It notes each director's background, principles and practices, and critical reception, using one representative production to illustrate each figure's work in detail (e.g., Ball's *Shrew*). Prosser correlates specific productions with trends and the effects of regionalism. The study has a bibliography and lists forty interviews.

262. *The Royal Shakespeare Theatre Company 1960–1963.* London: Max Reinhardt, 1964.

This anonymous commemoration of the fourth centennial of Shakespeare's birth documents crucial years of the revolution accomplished at the Stratford-upon-Avon Memorial Theatre by Peter Hall. It records cast lists, staff, and other production data, with numerous photographs of such distinctive productions as the cycle of the English history plays. Additionally there are short essays on the theatre company; on Shakespeare and the Modern Director by Peter Hall; and one on "Shakespeare and the Modern Playwright" by Robert Bolt. There is a section excerpting News Items, Editorials, Notices of Key Productions, etc.

263. **Rutter, Carol, *et al.*** *Clamorous Voices: Shakespeare's Women Today.* London: Women's Press, 1988. Repr. New York: Routledge, 1989.

These edited reports record leading actresses' remarks and conversations about their work at the Royal Shakespeare Company, covering their principal Shakespearean roles from 1978 to 1985 in plays directed by Michael Bogdanov, Adrian Noble, Trevor Nunn, Jonathan Miller, and Barry Kyle. Sinéad Cusack, Paola Dionisotti, Fiona Shaw, Juliet Stevenson, and Harriet Walter discuss their roles as Kate (*Shrew*), Rosalind (*As You Like It*), Isabella (*Measure*), Helena (*All's Well*), Lady Macbeth, and Imogen (*Cymbeline*), as stage realizations of modern feminist views of women's roles in Shakespeare. The tone is informal, without historical perspective and critical method, but permits practical illustrations of modern procedures in developing a performance. Many of the "discoveries" are traditional, but the sympathetic defense of Shakespeare's more assertive women characters is plausible, relevant to modern experience, and free of sociological and political dogmatism.

264. **Warren, Roger.** *Staging Shakespeare's Late Plays.* Oxford: Clarendon Press, 1990.

This survey is based on Peter Hall's 1988 National Theatre productions of *Cymbeline, Winter's Tale,* and *Tempest* at the Cottesloe, using a similar season in 1986 at Stratford, Ontario, as a foil (which allows Warren to add a chapter on *Pericles,* also performed at Stratford). Hall followed the innovations in the new Oxford collected edition, accepting the harsher view Stephen Orgel takes of Prospero in his edition of *Tempest.* Warren makes comparisons with effects in many other late-20th-century productions of the plays (by Nunn; Gaskill; Gielgud with Ashcroft; etc.), stressing Hall's darker, more serious, less decorative approach. Warren uses detailed accounts of key scenes to develop critical insights into textual meanings and characterizations. Ultimately Warren has some doubts about the new Oxford collected edition's initiatives. He particularly dislikes its "reconstruction" of the quarto *Pericles,* and he queries the plays' newly supposed ambiguities while he confirms Hall's sense of the plays as spiritual pilgrimages.

265. **Wells, Stanley.** *Royal Shakespeare: Four Major Productions at Stratford-upon-Avon.* Manchester: Manchester Univ. Press, 1976.

Wells prints four Furman University lectures. He describes Peter Hall's heavily-cut but virtuoso *Coriolanus* (Laurence Olivier, Edith Evans, Albert Finney, 1959) and his pro-Claudius and pro-Fortinbras *Hamlet* (David Warner, Brewster Mason, Tony Church, Glenda Jackson, 1965). He then reviews John Barton's Chekhovian *Twelfth Night* (Richard Pasco, Judi Dench, Donald Sinden, Tony Church, 1969–72) and his archaic, pro-Bolingbroke *Richard II* (Ian

Richardson alternating with Richard Pasco as Richard and Bolingbroke, Tony Church as John of Gaunt, 1973–74). Wells describes and interprets each production sympathetically.

See also nos. 53, 77, 78, 99, 112, 114, 126, 127, 129, 130, 133, 134, 135, 138, 139, 143, 149, 186, 187, 190, 192, 197, 198, 199, 215, 218, 219, 220, 284, 286.

5. Shakespeare on Film and Video

266. **Ball, Robert H.** *Shakespeare on Silent Film: A Strange and Eventful History.* New York: Theatre Arts 1968.

This illustrated survey of silent Shakespearean films from 1899 to 1929 provides exhaustive documentation for the productions: their making, character, and performance history. It explores primary sources and the factual history of all films within this category. There are extracts from shooting scripts and detailed scene-by-scene descriptions of major films. There are indexes of films and names, a bibliography, and full notes on the literary and visual sources. This encyclopedic but lucid account is a model of original research in an important but neglected field, essential for the study of Shakespeare in early cinema.

266a. **Boose, Linda. E., and Richard Burt, eds.** *Shakespeare, the Movie: Popularizing the Plays on Film, TV, and Video.* New York: Routledge, 1997.

The essays in this anthology include work by several established critics, such as Robert Hapgood, Barbara Hodgdon, and Kenneth Rothwell. Some essays deal with the film and television treatment of one script, including *Shrew, Richard III, Henry V, Hamlet, Othello, Lear, Shakespeare Wallah, Bugsy, My Own Private Idaho*, and *Prospero's Books*, but more general essays discuss Zeffirelli, animations, and gay versions. The approaches used include discussions of race, gender, politics, colonialisim, the impact of film techniques on scripts, and the effects of radical adaptation of plots and characters to fit modern views and analogues. The anthology provides a representative application of modern critical theory to the major examples of Shakespearean film down to Branagh and McKellen.

267. **Buchman, Lorne M.** *Still in Movement: Shakespeare on Screen.* Oxford: Oxford Univ. Press, 1991.

This theoretical approach to Shakespearean films explores the viewing of individual films as a series of unitary compositions. It illustrates detailed effects such as shifts in point of view and the visual interpretation of open and closed spaces. It includes a comparison of the storm scenes in the films of *Lear* by Brook and Kozintsev, and a discussion of the use of time in Welles' *Othello.* While discussing individual versions of particular effects seen as characteristic of cinematic treatments of Shakespeare, Buchman does not review the structure of whole scripts or performances, nor consolidate the work of particular directors.

268. **Bulman, J. C., and H. R. Coursen, eds.** *Shakespeare on Television: An Anthology of Essays and Reviews.* Hanover, N.H.: Univ. Press of New England, 1988.

This anthology contains numerous essays by leading authorities: Bernice Kliman, Marvin Rosenberg, Graham Holderness, Michael Mullin, James Lusardi, G. K. Hunter, Peter Saccio, etc. Part I covers broad issues. Part II contains essays on particular versions, grouped as tragedies, comedies, and histories. The book's major focus is on the BBC series, even in Part III, which is devoted to a chronological survey of representative videos, in which several versions of major plays appear. Each entry in Part III includes production company with date of completion, the date and agency of first showing, the main actors, and excerpts from a cross-section of major reviews. There is a bibliography and a videography of distributors. This book provides a comprehensive survey of the field.

269. **Collick, John.** *Shakespeare, Cinema and Society.* Manchester: Manchester Univ. Press, 1989.

This selective survey of Shakespearean films explores the economic and cultural factors affecting film versions of the plays. The first part sees silent film of Shakespeare as a derivative of Victorian bardolatry in the vein of Irving and Tree. It argues that Tree's early films use historical realism as the basis for creating a commercial/political industry illustrated later by Olivier's *Henry V* and the BBC television series. Part II offers a transcendental approach to filming Shakespeare, using symbolism, often Freudian, as in Reinhardt's *Dream*, Welles' *Othello*, and Jarman's *Tempest*. Following Bakhtin, Part III discusses Russian intellectualization of Shakespeare as an element of socialist art, and illustrated by Kozintsev's *Hamlet* and *Lear*. Part IV covers Japanese history and the warrior class in the films of Kurosawa, with Kurosawa's tendency to cultural determinism in *Throne of Blood* and *Ran*. The book seeks to validate an economic approach to Shakespearean film.

270. **Coursen, Herbert.** *Watching Shakespeare on Television.* Rutherford N. J.: Fairleigh Dickinson Univ. Press, 1993.

Coursen begins with a discussion of problems about televising Shakespeare's plays and audience responses to them. He then devotes chapters to film and video versions of various plays. He starts with versions of *Dream*, then proceeds to a chapter on *Hamlet* as seen in many different video renderings, such as those with Olivier, Kline, Schell, and Jacobi. He then moves on to the treatment of Gertrude by Zeffirelli. Other chapters discuss the editing of the various Shakespeare scripts; the case for a black Othello, as seen in Suzman's version and Nunn's; and Greenaway's *Prospero's Books*. Finally, he notes the increased accessibility of versions of the plays via video. A range of video examples is used throughout, in addition to the major selections noted.

271. **Davies, Anthony.** *Filming Shakespeare's Plays: The Adaptations of Laurence Olivier, Orson Welles, Peter Brook and Akira Kurosawa.* Cambridge: Cambridge Univ. Press, 1988.

Backed by Kozintsev's account of his *Hamlet* (in *Shakespeare: Time and Conscience*, London: Dennis Dobson, 1967), Davies distinguishes between theatrical space (seen as defined and static) and cinematic space (in which the camera can move without restraint). With the use of stills, he applies this distinction to Olivier's *Henry V*, *Hamlet*, and *Richard III*; to Welles' *Macbeth*, *Othello*, and *Chimes at Midnight*; to Brook's *Lear* and Kurosawa's *Throne of Blood*. Davies' initial model of the alternatives lies in Olivier's movement from one to the other in his film of *Henry V*. Davies suggests the effect of these films on Shakespeare production generally and compares the stage and film actors' techniques, finding in film a greater requirement of actor assimilation to the role. There is much useful close analysis of spatial relationships in Shakespeare production, whatever the firmness of the broad distinctions proposed between film and stage. See also A. Davies and S. Wells, eds. *Shakespeare and the Moving Image: The Plays on Film and Television* (1994).

272. **Donaldson, Peter S.** *Shakespearean Films/Shakespearean Directors.* Boston: Unwin Hyman, 1990.

This study covers six screen directors and seven films, which are analyzed as "retextualizations" of performances which permit closer scrutiny than stage productions. It uses Freudian and gender approaches, showing how Elizabethan conventions are refashioned on film. The critic correlates the character of the films with biographical facts about the directors' lives, with stress on Laurence Olivier's *Henry V* (the transmutation of the boy-actor role) and *Hamlet* (showing narcissism derived from the director's childhood); Akira Kurosawa's *Throne of Blood* (as allegory of East/West cinematic practice); Orson Welles' *Othello* (the screen mirroring fantasies of maternal insufficiency); Liz White's *Othello*, (African-American issues); Zeffirelli's *Romeo* (a homoeorotic, antipatriarchal interpretation); and Jean Luc Godard's *Lear* (as deconstruction). The study stresses readings of the films related to directors' biographies.

273. **Eckert, Charles W.** *Focus on Shakespearean Films.* Englewood Cliffs, N. J.: Prentice Hall, 1972.

This anthology consists of sections devoted to essays on major films (*Romeo, Caesar, Hamlet, Othello, Macbeth, Dream, Shrew, Richard III, Henry IV,* and *Henry V*) by noted critics (Mary McCarthy, Jack Jorgens, Gavin Lambert, Constance Brown, Dwight Macdonald, etc.). It includes an interview with Peter Brook about *Hamlet* and *Lear* on film. Values and concerns diverge widely; the collection displays views of cinematic Shakespeare from hostile to enthusiastic, subjective to professional. Some items are journalistic reflections of initial responses to films, illustrating the historical reception of featured productions. These views should be compared to those in a similar but far more recent anthology, by L. Boose and R. Burt, no. 266a, which updates the review of popular media versions of Shakespeare by using modern concerns about gender, race, colonialism, etc.

274. **Hallinan, Tim.** "Interview: Jonathan Miller on the [BBC] Shakespeare Plays." *Shakespeare Quarterly* 32 (1981): 134–45.

This interview with the second series producer of the BBC Shakespeare videos covers general problems of adaptation to television, including his own concerns as a director in connection with the distracting impact of modern archeology on his representations of ancient Rome in *Antony*, in which he used the model of Veronese's painting to recover Renaissance concepts of Rome for its staging. We also learn that Vermeer provided a similar, somber context for historical views of obedience as a social norm in *Shrew*. Miller also raises questions of anachronism concerning details in filming *Merchant* and in the series' modernized presentations of such rulers as Richard II, Lear, and Octavius Caesar. The interview provides helpful glimpses into local effects in Miller's middle phase of the series.

275. **Holderness, Graham.** "Radical Potentiality and Institutional Closure: Shakespeare in Film and Television." In Dollimore, no. 242: 182–201.

As a cultural materialist, Holderness notes tension between Shakespeare scripts and the film medium. He sees film as subversive of conservative literary values. Against Peter Hall's visual interpretations of the text at the R.S.C., Holderness argues that films such as Brook's *Lear* and Kurosawa's *Throne of Blood* disrupt both naturalism and literariness, achieving an alienation latent in the script. Holderness rejects the naturalism and coherence of BBC producers Jonathan Miller and Cedric Messina, favoring the relevance to Northern Ireland of Jane Howell's non-realistic *Henry VI* and *Richard III* in the BBC series. This approach to Shakespearean films is developed in S. Bennett, *Performing Nostalgia: Shifting Shakespeare and the Contemporary Past* (1996).

276. **Jorgens, Jack J.** *Shakespeare on Film.* Bloomington: Indiana Univ. Press, 1977.

This selective review of major Shakespearean films illustrates the principal considerations in transposing Shakespearean scripts to cinematic film, and argues for the modern medium as an independent, legitimate, and constructive source of insight into Shakespeare's art. It concentrates on the insights of major producers: Reinhardt, Hall, Zeffirelli, Welles, Olivier, Kurosawa, Polanski, and Konzintsev; and it applies close analysis to their principal feature films, with illustrative frames, stressing the tragedies, *Romeo, Macbeth, Othello, Hamlet,* and *Lear;* but with substantial attention to *Dream, Shrew, Henry IV, Henry V,* and *Richard III.* There is an extended appendix covering credits with scene outlines of the chosen films. The text coordinates discussion of the unique devices of film form to the broader aesthetic appreciation of Shakespearean scripts, and it provides a model for accommodating traditional critical insights to awareness of the effects of media on theatrical values.

277. **Kozintsev, Grigori.** *Shakespeare: Time and Conscience.* Trans. Joyce Vining. New York: Hill and Wang, 1966; London: Dennis Dobson, 1967.

While this text is primarily significant in documenting the development, making, and interpretation of Kozintsev's own films of *Hamlet* and *Lear,* it also reviews his precedents in such stage and film directors as Brook and Kurosawa, while placing greatest stress on the Russian critical and theatrical tradition in relation to Kosintsev's own procedures in filming these tragedies. The text contains substantial accounts of issues such as the use of location, periodization, visual symbolism, as well as nuances of characterization, textual intereperatation, and contemporary relevance. There is also a substantial section on *Henry IV.* The text is discontinuous and approaches a documentary anthology, but reveals Kozintsev's motives and methods.

278. **Manvell, Roger.** *Shakespeare and the Film.* New York: Praeger, 1971.

Manvell surveys the major Shakespearean films from 1929 to 1970, with chapters on Olivier, Welles, the Russians, Zeffirelli, Kurosawa, and late transpositions of stage productions into films such as Hall's *Dream* (1969). The book is primarily descriptive, with extracts from shooting scripts, and stress on contextual factors (funding, political considerations), production histories, and technical aspects (script writing, photography, casting). There is much useful primary material, presented in a rather disjointed, preliminary way, but covering major considerations in describing and evaluating film versions of Shakespeare.

279. **McKernan, Luke, and Olwen Terris, eds.** *Walking Shadows: Shakespeare in the National Film and Television Archive.* London: British Film Institute, 1994.

After a short history of filmed Shakespeare by Luke McKernan, the book goes through Shakespeare play by play, listing film and television versions, with production staff, cast, producing unit, location, and character of the print, followed by a descriptive and evaluative paragraph. It includes full productions, but also allusions, homages, parodies, borrowings, documentaries, newsreels, animations, commercials, dance, opera, and amateur film. Finally, Roberta Pearson and William Uricchio write on Vitagraph's Shakespearean productions, Tise Vahimagi on Shakespeare and the Hallmark Hall of Fame, and Olwen Terris on the BBC Shakespeare. The book lists relevant archives and libraries, with a bibliography, and name and title indexes. Though focused on one collection, it ranges from Tree's fragment of *John* (1899) to a video of Richard Eyre's *Richard III* at the National with McKellen (1992) and one of Branagh's R.S.C. *Hamlet* (1993). This filmography covers over 400 Shakespeare films and videos, many from non-English-speaking countries.

280. **Pilkington, Ace G.** *Screening Shakespeare From "Richard II" to "Henry V."* Newark: Univ. of Delaware Press, 1991.

Pilkington covers the factors shaping the BBC production of Shakespeare's second tetralogy of English history plays. He pays particular attention to the role of Cedric Messina as producer and David Giles as director, both favoring television realism as a concept over the theatrical artifice recognized by the script of *Henry V*. Pilkington stresses the consistent preference for close-ups over long-shots in the television versions. He concentrates on the principal actors in the series: Derek Jacobi (Richard II), Jon Finch (Bolingbroke/Henry IV), Antony Quayle (Falstaff), and David

Gwillim (Hal/Henry V). Two chapters use Olivier's *Henry V* and Welles' *Chimes at Midnight* as cinematic foils for the BBC versions. The book ends with a filmography and bibliography about the four productions. Throughout, Pilkington accepts the BBC premises about the character of television, despite criticism of the three later videos, which followed the initial critical success of Jacobi's distinctively harsh reading of Richard II as a tyrant.

281. **Richmond, Hugh Macrae.** "Shakespeare on Film. Angles of Vision: Recording *Much Ado* at the Restored Globe Theatre." *Shakespeare Bulletin* 15 (1997): 31–33.

The essay discusses problems in staging and recording performances of Shakespeare in the newly restored Globe Theatre in London. It identifies conflicts between the performance style dictated by an Elizabethan stage configuration and the conventions of modern television recording, with some resolutions for these disparities. The essay is based on experience in recording one of the first Elizabethan-style performances in this theatre on 15 July 1996.

282. **Sales, Roger, ed.** *Shakespeare in Perspective.* 2 vols. London: Ariel Books (BBC), 1982 & 1985.

Each of these two massive anthologies includes thirty-six essays "taken from radio and television commentaries" on the BBC TV Shakespeare series. The varied commentators include performers such as Peggy Ashcroft, Kenneth Branagh, Eleanor Bron, Judi Dench, Michael Hordern, Derek Jacobi, Barbara Jefford, Brewster Mason, Anthony Quayle, Roger Rees, Prunella Scales, Donald Sinden, Patrick Stewart, Dorothy Tutin, and Michael Wood. Other essays appear by Bridget Brophy, Anthony Burgess, Germaine Greer, Paul Johnson, Frank Kermode, John Mortimer, Dennis Potter, Stephen Spender, and Roy Strong. These short overviews, each devoted to one play, stress personal insights, not critical, scholarly, or technical issues. They are less focussed on BBC TV productions or on performance than is implied, but identify the Shakespearean approaches of theatrical authorities at the time of the BBC series.

283. *The Shakespeare Plays.* New York: Mayflower Books (BBC/Time-Life), 1979.

These single-play scripts of the BBC TV Shakespeare series use the text of Peter Alexander's edition, with production cuts indicated. Each volume has an introductory literary essay about the play by John Wilders; a short Preface by the series producer more directly related to performance; an essay by Henry Fenwick about the production in detail; a cast and crew list; a textual note; and about a dozen photographs, some in color. Fenwick's production notes illuminate interpretations, technical considerations, and other decisions, based on comments by cast and production personnel, including directors, script editors, costume designers, etc. Though slight as editions, these texts provide a reliable direct source for information about the production procedures used for each televised play.

284. **Silviria, Dale.** *Laurence Olivier and the Art of Film Making.* Cranbury, N. J.: Associated Univ. Presses, 1985.

Silviria is concerned with Olivier as a film director, chiefly of his three Shakespeare films: *Henry V, Hamlet,* and *Richard III.* Above all in *Henry V,* Silviria sees Olivier as a director creating an idealized world by slow tracking and formalistic direction, using actors stylized by setting, costume, staging, music, and montage. The physical detail of all three films is thoroughly discussed: for instance, the Expressionist vision of the castle at Elsinore, and the boldly symbolic settings of Richard's London. Olivier's own acting is defined in the varying styles of his Hamlet, measured against a background of critical interpretations, and in the dazzling opacity of his Richard's deliberately unrationalized psychology, which confirms the film's loss of moral perspective, matching *Hamlet*'s loss of political dimension.

285. **Willis, Susan.** *The BBC Shakespeare Plays: Making the Televised Canon.* Chapel Hill: Univ. of North Carolina Press, 1991.

Willis was an eyewitness observer of the BBC Shakespeare series. Part 1 covers the history of the series, with the change of producers from Cedric Messina to Jonathan Miller. Part 2 applies theories and procedures about the medium to the resulting changes in the series, showing how Miller moved away from Messina's conservative model with the aid of directors Elijah Moshinsky and Jane

Howell. Willis stresses the painterly models for Miller's *Shrew* (Vermeer), and *Antony* (Veronese), as with Moshinsky's *Love's Labour's* (Watteau). She contrasts stage and film conventions and notes problems resulting from the disparities between the professional, educational, and artistic interests of the U.S.A. and the U.K., including the refusal by British Equity to allow the BBC to cast the American actor James Earl Jones as Othello because he was not a U.K. professional. Part 3 exemplifies production procedures by specific allusions to *Troilus* (1981), *Errors* (1983), and *Titus* (1985). Appendices cover taping and transmission dates; a list of earlier BBC versions of Shakespeare; and a bibliography, with individual reviews. The book details directorial interpretations, with cuts and locations (using *As You Like It* and *Henry VIII* as examples). The book contextualizes the character and quality of all the videos it discusses.

See also nos. 22, 26, 99, 133, 135, 143, 218, 219, 222, 225, 227, 232, 240, 242, 245, 251, 254, 259, and 260.

E. Pedagogy

286. Barton, John. *Playing Shakespeare* (Videotape Series). Princeton: Films for the Humanities, 1984. Printed text with same title: London: Methuen, 1984.

Eleven videotapes (50 minutes each) cover workshops with the Royal Shakespeare Company, with directors Trevor Nunn, John Barton, and Terry Hands, working with actors Alan Howard, Jane Lapotaire, Ian McKellen, Michael Pennington, Patrick Stewart, and David Suchet. The printed text is based on these workshops, which discuss Speaking Shakespearean Verse (metrics and rhetoric); Preparing to Perform Shakespeare (developing scenes from the script of *Troilus*); The Two Traditions (Elizabethan stylized acting reconciled to modern naturalism, using *Hamlet, Coriolanus, Merchant,* and *Othello*); Using the Verse (with excerpts from *Henry V, Winter's Tale, Merchant, John, Antony, Troilus, Richard III*); Language and Character (with verbal subtleties from *Love's Labour's,*

Henry V, Caesar, Hamlet, Richard III, Antony, Merchant); Set Speeches and Soliloquies (with varied procedures and purposes); Irony and Ambiguity (in complex and ambivalent characters); Rehearsing the Text (the overt text and the concealed subtext in *Twelfth Night*); Passion and Coolness (moderation in Hamlet's advice to the actors); Exploring Character (chiefly Suchet and Stewart on the complexities of Shylock); Poetry and Hidden Poetry (close analysis of verse). Barton's directorial approach serves actors best, but visual and auditory work helps others to appreciate practical concerns in staging Shakespeare.

287. **Cohen, Robert.** *Acting in Shakespeare.* Mountain View, Cal.: Mayfield, 1991.

This textbook maps out a step-by-step course in teaching students how to perform Shakespearean roles in terms of current acting procedures and techniques. It discusses rhetorical formulas (antithesis, platforms, builds), costumes, physical movement, the handling of verse; and it provides thirty-two exemplary roles and treatments of them, ranging from Doll Tearsheet to Viola, Launcelot Gobbo to Richard II. As an introductory handbook it is accessible, and provides numerous local insights into the passages of script used as exercises.

288. **Davis, James E., and Ronald E. Salomone, eds.** *Teaching Shakespeare Today: Practical Approaches and Productive Strategies.* Urbana, Ill.: National Council of Teachers of English, 1993.

The core of this book consists of essays on performance approaches in the teaching of Shakespeare. Sections cover classroom use of student performance (61–106), and the classroom use of live actors, of films, of videotapes, and of computer programs (109–58). The book presents current classroom practice by experienced teachers at all levels throughout the U.S.A., confirming the pre-eminence of performance approaches in Shakespeare instruction. Though practical in emphasis, the text also includes allusions to current critical and sociological theory about Shakespeare's role in modern society. There is now a sequel: Ronald E. Salomone and James E. Davis, eds. *Teaching Shakespeare into the Twenty-First Century* (1997).

289. **Frey, Charles H.** *Experiencing Shakespeare: Essays on Text, Classroom and Performance.* Columbia: Univ. of Missouri Press, 1988.

These essays show a teacher experiencing the shift from New Criticism to more recent innovative ideas about the teaching and study of Shakespeare. A chapter reviews actors' concerns compared to those of teachers and scholars. Another provides an historical overview of the teaching of Shakespeare in America: its aims, functions, and methods, with some questioning of the effectiveness of performance in the classroom. These concerns evolve into an account of how study of rhetoric in grammar school may have affected Shakespeare's use of bombast as dramatist. This historical perspective illuminates analogous options in rhetorical training for the teachers of oral expression in the modern classroom.

290. **Grant, Cathy, ed.** *As You Like It: AudioVisual Shakespeare.* London: British Universities Film and Video Council, 1992.

This is a reference work by the British Shakespeare and Schools project (from the Shakespeare Institute of Education at Cambridge University). It includes introductory essays by Rex Gibson on teaching Shakespeare through film and video, David Olive on using video in teaching by performance, Raymond Ingram on aesthetic factors in the use of videos and the effects of filming scripts, and Murray Weston on copyright issues. The rest of the book is a reference guide to audio-visual versions of the plays and sonnets, and to background material for Shakespeare, mostly on video. There is a brief bibliography. While the focus is on outlets, materials, and formats in Britain, many items are also accessible in the U.S.A. (for U.S.A. sources see Rothwell, no. 22).

291. **Reynolds, Peter.** *Shakespeare: Text into Performance.* Harmondsworth: Penguin, 1991.

Reynolds outlines the procedures involved in transforming a script into a performance, from the points of view of the student, the actor, the director, the stage-designer, and the informed audience. The approach is highly practical and specific, covering casting, costumes, minor characters, props, sound effects, etc. Illustrations are provided from Shakespeare (chiefly *Richard III* and

Hamlet), and details are derived from current productions and methods. The text briefly establishes the principal considerations involved in staging a Shakespeare play.

292. **Richmond, Hugh M., Producer.** *Shakespeare and the Globe.* Video Documentary (30 minutes). Princeton: Films for the Humanities, 1986.

This videotape provides an overview of the visual material (paintings, designs, buildings, monuments, interviews, and performances) for Shakespeare students, stressing historical and theatrical contexts of Shakespeare's plays. It includes the notable opening of Olivier's *Henry V* film, staged in Elizabethan style, which re-creates a performance in the first Globe Theatre. Other excerpted performances show Shakespeare's precedents in ancient Greece and Rome, in the Middle Ages, and in the *commedia dell'arte*. These scenes explore, for example, the stereotype of the Braggart Soldier from Plautus to Falstaff. Traditional Morris Dances and modern student productions appear with visuals about Elizabethan theatre operation (and commentaries by scholar Andrew Gurr and actor/director Sam Wanamaker, who discuss the rebuilding of the Globe Theatre), and about English history, Elizabethan London, and Shakespeare's Warwickshire. Much visual material is covered.

293. **Richmond, Hugh M., Producer.** *Shakespeare's Globe Theatre Restored: Teaching By Performance.* Video Documentary (34 Minutes). Venice, Cal.: TMW Media, 1997.

This televised documentary is based on a visit to the newly restored Globe Theatre in Southwark, London, U.K. by a production of *Much Ado* staged by the University of California's Shakespeare Program in Berkeley. This group rehearsed and staged one of the first Elizabethan-style performances on the new stage, before an invited audience, on 15 July 1996. The documentary records the company's rehearsals on this stage, the live performance before an invited audience, and the review of what was learned from the production. It records expositions about the International Shakespeare Globe Centre by its Chief Executive, Michael Holden; by its Artistic Director, Mark Rylance; by its Director of Research, Andrew Gurr; and by its Director of Education, Patrick Spottiswoode. The documentary discusses and illustrates such issues as the new theatre's acoustics and the spatial challenges provided by the galleries and the two large down-stage pillars. This program is a resource for groups wishing to stage a performance on the new Globe's stage, and for all interested in studying how productions can operate in such a space.

See also nos. 22, 236, and journals such as Shakespeare Bulletin; Shakespeare in the Classroom; Shakespeare Quarterly; Shakespeare on Film Newsletter; Shakespeare Survey; and Studies in Teaching the Middle Ages and the Renaissance.

INDEX I
AUTHORS AND EDITORS
Please note that authors may also appear in the subject index.

Adams, John Cranford, 68, 82, 151.
Adams, Joseph Quincy, 73.
Addenbrooke, David, 225.
Agate, James, 212.
Allen, Shirley S., 200.
Archer, William, 158.
Armstrong, William A., 27, 154.
Arnott, James Fullerton, 125.
Aronson, Arnold, 196.
Arundell, D., 200.
Ashcroft, Peggy, 187, 225, 282.
Ashley, Leonard R. N., 175.
Astington, John H., 66, 69.
Avery, Emmett, 159.

Babula, William, 226.
Baker, Herschel, 2, 176.
Baldwin, Thomas W., 87, 105, 151.
Ball, Robert H., 171, 260, 266.
Barish, Jonas, 28.
Barker, Richard H., 175.
Barroll, J. Leeds, 55.
Barton, Anne (Righter), 111, 113, 260.
Barton, John, 22, 286.
Baskervill, C. R., 29.
Bate, Jonathan, 126.
Beauman, Sally, 186.
Beckerman, Bernard, 13, 111, 135, 138, 150.
Bennett, Susan, 275.
Bentley, Gerald Eades, 14, 30, 31, 40, 84, 114, 154, 155.
Berger, Harry, 28, 153.
Bergeron, David M., 32, 122.
Berry, Herbert, 65, 74.
Berry, Ralph, 88, 127, 150, 202, 227, 228.
Bevington, David, 33, 89.

Billington, Michael, 187.
Blatherwick, Simon, 75, 78.
Blaydes, Sophia B., 178.
Blayney, Peter W. M., 4, 36a.
Boaden, James, 176.
Bogdanov, Michael, 228, 229.
Bolt, Robert, 262.
Booth, Michael R., 202.
Booth, Stephen, 138.
Boose, Linda E., 266a, 273.
Bordinat, Philip, 178.
Bowmer, Angus, 207, 230.
Bradbrook, Muriel, 34, 90, 154, 260.
Bradley, David, 35.
Branagh, Kenneth, 258, 282.
Branham, George C., 160.
Braunmuller, Albert, 43, 150.
Brissenden, Alan, 91.
Bristol, Michael D., 36a.
Brockbank, Philip, 231.
Bron, Eleanor, 282.
Brophy, Bridget, 282.
Brook, Peter, 129, 232, 234, 273.
Brown, Constance, 273.
Brown, Ivor, 233.
Brown, John Russell, 138, 150, 154, 234, 235, 258.
Brown, Langdon, 256.
Brownstein, Oscar, 74.
Buchman, Lorne M., 267.
Bullough, Geoffrey, 15.
Bulman, James C., 236, 268.
Bulwer, John, 53.
Burgess, Anthony, 282.
Burnim, Kalman A., 167, 184.
Burt, Richard, 266a, 273.
Butler, Martin, 155.
Byrne, M. St. Claire, 260.

Index

Campbell, Lily B., 66.
Carlisle, Carol J., 188.
Carroll, Lewis, 140.
Carson, Neil, 49.
Cary, Cecile, 42.
Chambers, E. K., 16, 17, 34, 40, 46, 71.
Champion, Larry, 196.
Chandler, Pamela, 198.
Charney, Maurice, 135, 150.
Cibber, Colley, 175.
Clare, J., 39.
Clark, George, 134.
Clarke, Mary, 198.
Clayton, Thomas, 150.
Cleary, James W., 53.
Clubb, L. G., 54.
Cochrane, Claire, 213.
Coghill, Nevill, 103, 260.
Cohen, Robert, 287.
Cohn, Ruby, 189.
Colley, John Scott, 97.
Collick, John, 269.
Conolly, Leonard W., 128.
Cook, Anne Jennalie, 36, 36a.
Cooper, Roberta Krensky, 237.
Coursen, Herbert, 238, 239, 268, 270.
Coven, Brenda, 252.
Cox, John D., 36a.
Craig, Edward, 201.
Craik, T. W., 38.
Crane, Ronald S., 166.
Croft, Michael, 250.
Crosse, Gordon, 190.
Crowl, Samuel, 240.
Cusack, Sinéad, 231, 263.

Dachlager, Earl, 196.
Daniell, David, 26.
David, Richard, 241.
Davies, Anthony, 271.
Davies, W. Robertson, 92.
Davis, Antony, 126.

Davis, James E., 288.
Davis, Thomas, 161.
Davis, Tracy C., 179.
Dawson, Anthony B., 129, 236.
De Bank, C., 93.
Dench, Judi, 126, 282.
Dent, Robert W., 175.
Dessen, Alan C., 26, 37, 38, 78, 94, 135, 150, 236.
Dionisotti, Paula, 263.
Dobbs, Brian, 130.
Dobson, Michael, 173.
Dollimore, Jonathan, 242, 275.
Donaldson, Peter S., 272.
Donawerth, Jane L., 42.
Donnellan, Declan, 228.
Donohue, Joseph W., 162.
Doran, John, 163.
Doran, Madeleine, 18.
Downer, Alan S., 177, 260.
Downes, John, 164.
Drakakis, John, 250.
Drew-Bear, Annette, 38.
Dunn, Esther Cloudman, 131.
Dunsworth, Felicity, 36a.
Dusinberre, Juliet, 236.
Dutton, Richard, 36a, 39.

Eccles, Christina, 76.
Eccles, Mark, 40.
Eckert, Charles W., 273.
Edmond, Mary, 178.
Edwards, Philip, 111, 155.
Egan, Gabriel, 29.
Elliott, John R., 36a.
Ellis, Ruth, 186.
Ellrodt, Robert, 26.
Elton, W. R., 26.
Engle, Ron, 243.
Epp, Garrett P. J., 36a.
Evans, G. Blakemore, 2, 143.
Ewbank, Inga-Stina, 26, 126, 150.

Farjeon, Herbert, 214.

Felver, C. S., 96.
Fenwick, Henry, 283.
Feuillerat, Albert, 41.
Ffrench, Yvonne, 185.
Findlater, Richard, 170, 171.
Fish, Stanley, 102,
Fitzgerald, Percy, 176.
Fitzpatrick, Tim, 83.
Fitzsimmons, Raymond, 179.
Flatter, Richard, 95.
Flecknoe, Richard, 156.
Fletcher, Kyle, 201.
Foakes, Reginald A., 42, 43, 49, 67, 126, 150.
Fone, B. R. S., 175.
Forster, John, 158.
Fotheringham, Richard, 114.
Foulkes, Richard, 202.
Frey, Charles H., 289.
Furness, H. H., 8.

Gay, Penny, 244.
Genest, John, 165.
Gibson, Rex, 290.
Gielgud, John, 245.
Gilbert, Miriam, 138.
Gildon, Charles, 180.
Goldman, Michael, 132, 138, 150.
Goldsmith, Oliver, 140.
Goldsmith, Robert, 96.
Gooch, Bryan N. S., 97.
Gosson, Stephen, 42, 44.
Grant, Cathy, 290.
Granville-Barker, Harley, 137, 188, 191, 195, 205, 210, 221, 245.
Graves, R. B., 98.
Gray, Charles H., 166.
Grebanier, Bernard, 133.
Greenblatt, Stephen, 3, 110.
Greenwald, Michael L., 246.
Greene, John, 50.
Greer, Germaine, 282.
Greg, Walter W., 34, 45.

Gurr, Andrew, 19, 20, 36, 46, 75, 77, 78, 150, 292, 293.
Guthrie, Tyrone, 215.

Halio, Jay, 111, 170, 247.
Hall, Peter, 228, 248, 262, 264.
Hallinan, Tim, 274.
Halstead, William P., 134.
Hapgood, Robert, 26, 99, 135, 266a.
Harbage, Alfred, 36, 42, 135.
Hart, Alfred, 47, 107.
Harwood, Ronald, 216.
Hasler, Jorg, 100.
Hattaway, Michael, 43, 48.
Hawkes, Terence, 135.
Hazleton, Nancy J. Doran, 202.
Hazlitt, William C., 156, 158, 162, 181.
Heinemann, Margaret, 242.
Henderson, Diana E., 36a.
Henslowe, Philip, 13, 49, 76, 83.
Heywood, Thomas, 42, 50.
Higgins, Anne, 36a.
Highfill, Philip, 167.
Hildy, Franklin J., 78, 249.
Hill, Errol, 192.
Hillebrand, Harold N., 179.
Hinman, Charlton, 4, 95.
Hirsh, James, 103.
Hodgdon, Barbara, 107, 135, 236, 266a.
Hodges, Walter, 71, 78, 79, 80, 82.
Hodgson, John, 250.
Hogan, Charles B., 159, 168.
Holbein, Woodrow L., 196.
Holderness, Graham, 242, 250, 268, 275.
Holland, Peter, 126, 251.
Holmes, Martin, 101.
Homan, Sidney, 107, 135.
Hordern, Michael, 282.
Hornbrook, David, 250.
Hosley, Richard, 55, 68, 69, 71, 74, 82, 84, 154.

Hotson, Leslie, 81, 96, 169.
Houtchens, Lawrence and Carolyn W., 182.
Howard, Jean E., 102.
Howe, Elizabeth, 170.
Howe, P. P., 181.
Hughes, Alan, 203.
Hunt, Albert, 252.
Hunt, Hugh, 198,
Hunt, Leigh, 158, 182.
Hunter, G. K., 268.

Ingram, Raymond, 290.
Ingram, William, 51.
Irving, Laurence, 203.
Isaacs, J., 107.

Jackson, M. P., 26.
Jackson, Russell, 26, 126, 231.
Jacobi, Derek, 282.
Jacobs, Henry E., 193.
Jamieson, Michael, 128, 154.
Jefford, Barbara, 282.
Jewkes, Wilfred T., 52.
Johnson, Claudia, 193.
Johnson, Paul, 282.
Jones, Emrys, 103, 111.
Jorgens, Jack J., 273, 276.
Joseph, Bertram L., 53.
Jowett, John, 155.

Kahn, Michael, 228.
Kahrl, George M., 184.
Kastan, David Scott, 36a.
Kay, Carol M., 196.
Kaye, F. B., 166.
Kelly, F. M., 136.
Kemble, John P., 183.
Kemp, Thomas C., 194.
Kendall, Alan, 184.
Kennedy, Dennis, 191, 195, 236.
Kermode, Frank, 2, 282.
Kernan, Alvin, 55, 104, 110.
Kernodle, George, 70.

King, Christine, 253.
King, T. J., 105, 106.
Kipling, Gordon, 36a.
Klein, David, 107.
Kliman, Bernice, 268.
Knight, G. Wilson, 217.
Knowles, Richard, 236.
Knutson. Roslyn L., 36a, 108.
Kolin, Phip C., 196.
Koon, Helene W., 205.
Kozintsev, Grigori, 277.
Kott, Jan, 254.

Lambert, Gavin, 273.
Langhans, Edward A., 167.
Lanier, Douglas, 236.
Lavin, J. A., 84.
Levin, Richard, 140.
Lea, Kathleen Marguerite, 54.
Leach, Clifford, 260.
Leaming, Barbara, 255.
Leggatt, Alexander, 55, 157.
Leiter, Samuel L., 256.
Levin, Harry, 2, 26.
Levine, Linda, 111a.
Lewes, George, 158.
Limouse, Henry S., 42.
Linthicum, M. C., 56.
Liston, William T., 143.
Londré, Felicia Hardison, 243, 256, 257.
Long, John H., 97.
Longhurst, Derek, 250.
Lowe, Robert W., 125, 158.
Lower, Charles B., 196.
Lusardi, James, 268.

Macdonald, Dwight, 273.
MacIntyre, Jean, 36a.
MacMinn, George, 204.
Macready, William Charles, 177.
Madden, Patricia, 196.
Mansfield, Alan, 136.
Manvell, Roger, 185, 278.

Marker, L. L., 42.
Marowitz, Charles, 258.
Marsden, Jean, 160.
Marshall, Norman, 137.
Mason, Brewster, 282.
Masten, Jeffrey, 36a.
Maufort, Marc, 257.
Mazer, Cary M., 205, 236.
McBean, Angus, 186, 198, 233.
McCarthy, Mary, 273.
McCullough, Christopher, 250.
McGuire, Philip C., 109, 138.
McKernan, Luke, 279.
McLuskie, Kathleen E., 36a, 155.
McNeir, Waldo, 196.
Mehl, Dieter, 26, 57.
Melzer, Annabelle Henkin, 22.
Merchant, W. Moelwyn, 139, 202.
Miller, John, 218, 245.
Miller, Jonathan, 247, 250, 256, 259, 263, 274, 275, 285.
Miller, Tice, 256.
Montrose, Louis, 104, 110.
Morseberger, Robert E., 58.
Mortimer, John, 282.
Mowat, Barbara A., 36a.
Muir, Kenneth, 26, 111, 170.
Mullin, Michael, 197, 256, 268.
Mulryne, J. R., 54.
Muriello, Karen M., 197.

Nagler, Alois, 82.
Nalley, Sarah, 196.
Nash, George, 206.
Nelson, Alan H., 36a, 69.
Newlyn, Jeanne, 260.
Newton, Stella Mary, 59.
Nungezer, Edwin, 40.
Nunn, Trevor, 228.

Odell, George C. D., 171, 176.
Olivier, Sir Laurence, 219.
Omans, Stuart E., 196.
Onions, C. T., 21.

Orange, Linwood E., 196.
Orgel, Stephen, 110, 111, 111a, 264.
Orrell, John, 36a, 66, 70, 75, 77, 78, 83.
Osborne, Laurie, 236.

Palmer, D. J., 111, 170.
Papp, Joseph, 6.
Parry, Graham, 36a.
Payne, Ben Iden, 207, 230.
Pearson, Hesketh, 208.
Pearson, Roberta, 279.
Peat, Derek, 150.
Pennington, Michael, 229, 231.
Phillips, Robin, 228.
Pilkington, Ace G., 280.
Poel, William, 137, 191, 195, 205, 207, 209, 211, 221, 222, 232, 234, 246, 249.
Pollock, Sir Frederick, 177.
Pope, W. J. Macqueen, 130.
Potter, Dennis, 282.
Potter, John 166.
Potter, Lois, 155, 260.
Price, Joseph G., 260.
Prosser, William L., 261.

Quayle, Anthony, 186, 233, 282.
Quiller-Couch, Arthur, 7.

Rapollo. Joseph P., 196.
Rasmussen, Eric, 36a.
Rees, Roger, 282.
Reeves, Geoffrey, 252.
Reynolds, G. F., 68.
Reynolds, Peter, 291.
Richman, David, 112.
Richmond, Hugh M., 78, 150, 281, 292, 293.
Rickert, R. T., 49.
Righter, Anne (Barton), 111, 113, 260.
Ringler, William A., 114, 154.
Roberts, Jeanne A., 111, 170.

Index

Roberts, Peter, 198.
Robinson, John W., 125.
Rogers, Houston, 198.
Rood, Arnold, 201.
Rose, Mark, 103.
Rosenberg, Marvin, 42, 138, 147, 150, 154, 268.
Rosenfeld, Sybil, 260.
Rothwell, Kenneth, 22, 290.
Rowell, George, 198.
Rutter, Carol Chillinton, 76, 263.

Saccio, Peter, 268.
Salomone. Ronald E., 288.
Sales, Roger, 282.
Salgado, Gamini, 140.
Salter, Denis, 236.
Samuelson, David, 138.
Saunders, J. W., 154.
Scales, Prunella, 282.
Schmidgall, Gary, 141.
Schoenbaum, Samuel, 23.
Schoester, Robert, 172.
Seefe, Adele, 111.
Seng, Peter J., 97.
Shapiro, Michael, 60.
Shattuck, Charles H., 2, 143, 144, 145, 183.
Shaw, Fiona, 263.
Shaw, G. B., 210.
Shewring, Margaret, 54.
Shirley, Frances Ann, 115, 260.
Shurgot, M. W., 88.
Sinden, Donald, 282.
Silviria, Dale, 284.
Sinfield, Alan, 242, 250.
Skura, Meredith A., 116.
Slater, Ann Pasternak, 117.
Smallwood, Robert, 26, 126, 231.
Smith, Hallett, 2.
Smith, Irwin, 71, 84.
Smith, Warren D., 71, 118.
Somerset, Alan, 61.
Southern, Richard, 168.

Speaight, Robert, 146, 211.
Spencer, Christopher, 173.
Spencer, Hazelton, 173.
Spender, Stephen, 282.
Spevack, Marvin, 24.
Sprague, Arthur Colby, 119, 146, 147, 148, 220, 260.
Sprigg, Douglas, 138.
Stallybrass, Peter, 92, 111a.
Stamm, Rudolph, 149, 260.
Sternfeld, F. W., 97.
Stevens, David, 62.
Stevenson, Juliet, 263.
Stewart, Patrick, 282.
Stinson, James, 71.
Stone, G. W., 184.
Stopes, Charlotte C., 120.
Strehler, Giorgio, 228.
Streitberger, W. R., 36a.
Strong, Roy, 282.
Styan, John L., 25, 78, 121, 138, 150, 221.
Summers, Montague, 164, 173.
Swander, Homer, 150.

Taborski, Boleslaw, 254.
Taylor, Gary, 153, 155.
Terris, Olwen, 279.
Thais, Christopher J., 196.
Thaler, A., 109.
Thatcher, David, 97.
Thompson, Ann, 250.
Thompson, Marvin and Ruth, 150.
Thomson, Peter, 26, 36a, 85, 126.
Toulmin, Mary D., 196.
Trewin, John C., 146, 220, 222, 223, 260.
Tucker, Patrick, 95.
Tutin, Dorothy, 282.

Uricchio, William, 279.

Vahimagi, Tise, 279.
Vallillo, Stephen M., 224.

Vesnezky, Alice S., 122.
Vining, Joyce, 277.

Waldo, Tommy Ruth, 135.
Walter, Harriet, 263.
Warren, Roger, 26, 264.
Watermeier, Daniel J., 243, 256.
Watkins, Ronald, 151.
Wearing, J. P., 128, 199.
Weimann, Robert, 110, 111, 123.
Wells, Stanley, 26, 128, 193, 260, 264, 265, 271.
Welsford, Enid, 63.
Werstine, Paul, 36a.
Weston, Murray, 290.
White, Beatrice, 16.
White, Paul W., 36a.
Wickham, Glynne, 72, 74, 150.
Wiggins, Martin, 126.
Wilders, John, 250, 283.
Wiles, David, 63, 124.
Williams, Clifford, 225.
Williams, D., 232.
Williams, Harcourt, 198, 249.
Williams, Raymond, 242.
Williams, Simon, 202.
Williamson, Audrey, 198.
Williamson, Jane, 260.
Willis, Susan, 285.
Wilson, Edwin, 210.
Wilson, F. P., 154.
Wilson, Jean, 86.
Wilson, John Dover, 7.
Winter, William, 152.
Winters, Yvor, 28.
Wood, Michael, 282.
Wood, Roger, 198.
Worthen, W. B., 153, 236.
Wright, James, 174.
Wright, Louis B., 154.
Wright, William Aldis, 134.

Yates, Frances, 64.

Zimmerman, Susan, 111.

INDEX II
SUBJECTS
Please note that authors may also appear in the author index.

act & scene divisions, 32, 37, 38, 44, 52, 60, 85, 103, 114, 266, 276.
acting, 19, 25, 36a, 42, 48, 50, 53, 60, 82, 85, 87, 89, 92, 93, 116, 117, 121, 126, 133, 138, 141, 147, 151, 154, 174, 176, 179, 180, 219, 230, 233, 235, 245, 246, 284, 286, 287, 291.
actors (see also individual names), 25, 26, 31, 33, 34, 36, 40, 42, 45, 46, 50, 55, 87, 105, 111, 114, 116, 132, 135, 146, 152, 154, 156, 164, 167, 192, 197, 199, 286, 289, 291.
actors' parts, 45, 87.
actresses (see also individual names), 144, 146, 147, 161, 162, 164, 170, 190, 192, 196, 199, 231, 244, 263.
adaptations, 159, 160, 173, 188, 189, 247, 258, 271, 274.
African (black) roles, 133, 146, 188, 192, 196, 224, 237, 266a, 270, 272 (see *Antony & Cleopatra, Othello, Titus Andronicus*).
Aikens, Maria, 238.
Aldridge, Ira, 192.
Aldwych theatre, 197.
Alexander, Bill, 228, 238.
Alexander, Peter, 283.
Alleyn, Edward, 19, 34, 43, 50, 101.
America (see also individual names), 131, 143, 144, 146, 152, 171, 172, 188, 192, 196, 204, 207, 215, 216, 224, 226, 228, 230, 237, 247, 249, 257, 261, 272, 285, 288, 289.
Andrews, Harry, 233.
Antoon, A. J., 239, 251.

Aristotle, 178.
Armin, Robert, 124.
Artaud, Antonin, 258.
Ashcroft, Peggy, 187, 225, 233, 244, 245, 246, 248, 264, 282.
Ashland (Oregon), 207, 230.
asides, 95, 102, 118, 119, 121, 150, 223.
Atkins, Robert, 198.
audiences, 19, 25, 27, 29, 35, 36, 36a, 37, 47, 50, 59, 72, 74, 77, 81, 88, 92, 102, 111, 112, 113, 116, 118, 119, 132, 135, 149, 154, 155, 157, 163, 164, 186, 200, 225, 227, 247, 257, 258, 260, 291.
Augustine, Saint, 28.

Bakhtin, Mikhail, 269.
Bale, John, 33.
Ball, William, 261.
Banqueting Hall (Whitehall), 20, 70.
Barrett, George, 144.
Barry, Elizabeth, 163, 169, 180.
Barrymore family, 146.
Barton, John, 22, 148, 186, 187, 225, 235, 239, 241, 244, 246, 247, 258, 265, 286.
Baylis, Lilian, 146.
BBC Shakespeare series, 239, 250, 259, 268, 269, 274, 275, 279, 280, 282, 283, 285.
Bear Gardens, 169.
Beaumont, Francis, 87.
Beckett, Samuel, 150, 189; *Endgame*, 254.
Benson, Frank, 186, 190, 208, 222.
Bernhardt, Sarah, 144.

Betterton, Thomas, 130, 161, 163, 164, 171, 178, 180.
bibliography, 22, 60, 62, 97, 125, 128, 172, 193, 201, 226, 253, & p. 18.
Birmingham Repertory, 194, 213.
Birmingham (Alabama), 196.
black, see African.
Blackfriars Theatre, 27, 29, 43, 70, 82, 84, 107, 120, 174.
blocking, 25, 60, 89, 118, 121, 123, 135.
Bloom, Claire, 190.
Boar's Head Theatre, 43, 65.
Bogdanov, Michael, 195, 228, 229, 238, 240, 247, 250, 263.
Bond, Edward, 250.
Booth, Barton, 163.
Booth, Edwin, 144, 196, 205.
Booth, Junius Brutus, 144, 158.
Bowe, John, 231.
Bowmer, Angus, 207, 230.
boy actors, 16, 31, 34, 35, 42, 43, 44, 92, 111a, 114, 121, 141, 151, 163, 174, 236, 272.
Branagh, K., 239, 258, 266a, 279.
Brecht, Bertolt, 129, 189, 195, 227, 232, 242, 250, 254, 258.
Brierly, David, 225.
Bright, Timothy, 42.
Brome, Richard, 155.
Bron, Eleanor, 282.
Brook, Peter, 129, 137, 153, 186, 195, 221, 227, 228, 233, 234, 241, 242, 247, 248, 252, 254, 267, 271, 273, 275, 277.
Brown, John Russell, 258.
Bruce, Brenda, 231.
Brunton, Anne, 144.
Bugsy, 266a.
Bull Theatre, 43.
Bulwer's *Chironomia*, 53.
Burbage, James, 72, 74, 120.
Burbage, Richard, 19, 43, 101, 120.

burlesques of Shakespeare, 193.
Bury, John, 225.

California, 131, 172, 205, 292, 293.
Callow, Simon, 153.
Cambridge University, 36a, 69, 81, 246, 250.
Campbell, Mrs. Patrick, 211.
Carnegie Tech., 206.
Carroll, Lewis, 140.
Casson, Louis, 214.
casting, 31, 33, 35, 60, 87, 105, 114, 127, 168, 192, 197, 198, 199, 203, 220, 230, 256, 262, 279, 283, 284, 285, 291.
censorship and theatre closures, 16, 28, 30, 36a, 39, 44, 72, 125, 155, 156, 169, 174.
ceremonies, 89.
Chamberlain's Men, 46.
Chancery, 169.
Charles I, 32.
Charles II, 164.
Charleston, 196.
Chekhov, Anton, 246, 265.
Cheek by Jowl, 228, 251.
chronicle plays, 33.
Church, Tony, 231, 265.
Cibber, Colley, 161, 163, 171, 175, 210.
clowns, see fools.
Cockpit Theatre, 43, 70.
Cole, Edward, 261.
collaboration, 30.
college hall screens, 69.
colonialism, 266a.
commedia dell'arte, 54, 292.
companies (of actors), 16, 28, 30, 31, 34, 35, 43, 46, 55, 85, 87, 108, 155, 170, 192, 230.
Condell, Henry, 4.
Cooke, George Frederick, 144, 176.
costumes, 36a, 38, 56, 59, 60, 89, 93, 94, 111a, 114, 117, 135, 136, 140,

146, 157, 171, 177, 187, 211, 216, 220, 285, 287, 291.
court, 36a, 63, 66, 70, 81, 82, 104, 155.
Covent Garden, 161.
Cox, Brian, 153.
Craig, Gordon, 137, 146, 195, 201, 204, 206, 213, 233.
Crane, Ralph, 154.
Cultural Materialism, 39, 242, 250, 275.
Curtain Theatre, 43, 51, 82.
curtains, 27, 81.
Cusack, Sinéad, 231, 263.
Cushman, Charlotte, 144, 146, 196, 205.

Daly, Augustin, 144, 152.
dance, 20, 21, 22, 91, 93, 97, 124, 180, 279, 292.
Daniels, Ron, 238.
Davenant, Sir William, 66, 155, 164, 169, 170, 173, 178, 188.
Davenport, E. L., 144.
Davis, Henrietta, 192.
Dee, John, 64.
Dekker, Thomas, 107, 155.
Dench, Judi, 126, 241, 265.
Derby's Men, 46.
Dionisotti, Paola, 263.
disguises, 28, 117, 260.
Donellan, Declan, 228.
doors, 106.
doubling, 31, 33, 35, 60, 105, 114, 127, 138, 237.
Dreyfuss, Richard, 196.
Drury Lane Theatre, 130, 175.
Dryden, John, 168, 173, 174.
Duke's Company, 170.
dumb shows, 57, 121.
duration of performances, 27, 35, 47.

Edward III, 48.
Elizabeth I, 32, 34, 39.

English Shakespeare Company, 229, 251.
entrances (& exits), 35, 118.
Equity, 144, 243, 285.
Essex, Earl of, 39.
Evans, Edith, 198, 223, 265.
Eyre, Richard, 238, 251, 279.

Fairbanks, Douglas, 269.
Falstaff, Sir John, 33, 39, 63, 124, 132, 220, 280, 292.
Federal Theatre Project, 172, 192, 224, 255.
feminism, 239, 242, 244, 250, 263.
Field, Nathan, 43.
fights, duels, etc., 38, 58, 154.
films, 21, 26, 99, 133, 135, 143, 146, 153, 218, 219, 225, 227, 239, 240, 242, 245, 251, 254, 259, 266–285, 288.
Finch, Jon, 280.
Finney, Albert, 248, 265.
Fletcher, Alan, 261.
Fletcher, John, 87, 155.
Florida, 172, 196.
Fludd, Robert, *Art of Memory*, 64.
Folger Shakespeare Library, 4, 9.
fools (and clowns; see also individual names), 20, 43, 63, 96, 116, 123, 124, 157, 161.
Foote, Samuel, 163.
Forbes-Robertson, Johnston, 210.
Ford, John, 155.
Forrest, Edwin, 144, 158.
Fortune Theatre, 20, 43, 83.
Foucault, Michel, 236, 242.
Freedman, Gerald, 261.
Freud, Sigmund, 116, 254, 269, 272.
Furby, Tim, 251.

Gaiety Theatre (Manchester), 207.
Garrick, David, 126, 145, 161, 162, 163, 167, 171, 184, 188.
Gaskill, William, 264.

gender, 44, 92, 110, 111a, 236, 244, 257, 266a, 272.
gesture, 38, 53, 89, 121, 180, 235.
Gibbon and Lisle's Tennis Courts, 169.
Gielgud, John, 133, 187, 188, 190, 233, 244, 245, 248, 264.
Giles, David, 280.
Globe Theatre (first), 13, 16, 20, 43, 65, 68, 70, 74, 75, 77, 78, 79, 81, 83, 86, 110, 116, 120, 154, 157, 260.
Globe Theatre (second), 74, 75, 77, 78, 79, 80, 83, 157.
Globe Theatre (modern), 64, 78, 121, 143, 250, 281, 292, 293.
Godard, Jean-Luc, 272.
Goethe, Johann W. von, 189.
Gold Rush, 204.
Gorboduc, 57.
Gosson, Stephen, *School of Abuse*, 42, 44.
Granville, George, *Jew of Venice*, 173.
Granville-Barker, Harley, 137, 188, 191, 194, 195, 204, 210, 221, 245.
Greek classical theatre, 292.
Greenaway, Peter, *Prospero's Books*, 236, 245, 270.
Greene, John, *Refutation of Apology for Actors*, 50.
Greene, Robert, 69; *Orlando Furioso*, 45.
Greet, Ben, 191, 198.
Guinness, Alec, 190.
Guthrie, Tyrone, 137, 146, 190, 195, 198, 214, 215, 221, 233, 247, 249.
Gwillim, David, 280.
Gwyn, Nell, 170.

Hackett, James, 144.
hall screens, 69.
Hall, Peter, 137, 148, 186, 187, 195, 228, 235, 238, 240, 242, 247, 248, 250, 258, 262, 264, 265, 275, 276, 278.
Hallam family, 144.
Hallmark Hall of Fame, 279.
Hammersmith (theatre), 216.
Hands, Terry, 239, 241, 250, 286.
Hare, David, 238.
Hauptmann, Gerhart, 189.
Haymarket Theatre, 212.
Helpman, Robert, 233.
Hemminge, John, 4.
Henry VIII's Calais banquet tent, 70, 74.
Henslowe, Philip, 13, 49, 76, 83.
Herkomer, Herbert, 260.
Hewlett, James, 146.
Heywood, Thomas,155; *Apology for Actors*, 42, 50.
His Majesty's Theatre, 212 (see Tree).
Holden, Michael, 293.
Hollar, Wenceslaus, 80, 83.
homosexuality, 111a, 266a.
Hope Theatre, 43.
Hopkins, Anthony, 129.
Houseman, John, 237.
Houston, 196.
Howard, Alan, 286.
Howell, Jane, 239, 275, 285.
Hunsdon's Men, 46.
Hutchings, Geoffrey, 231.
Hytner, Nicolas, 238.

Illinois, Univ. of, 197.
inns as theatres, 43, 65, 70, 72, 73, 169.
interludes, 123.
Irving, Henry, 129, 146, 171, 190, 202, 203, 205, 208, 210, 269.
Ivory, James, 22.

Jackson, Barry, 194, 213, 221.
Jackson, Glenda, 265.

Index

Jackson, Nagle, 261.
Jacobean drama (see also individual names), 28, 47, 52, 56, 57, 59, 114, 154, 157, 174.
Jacobi, Derek, 239, 270, 280.
James I, 32, 104.
Jarman, Derek, 240, 269.
Jolly, George, 169.
Jones, Gemma, 231.
Jones, Inigo, 64, 66, 72, 77; Banqueting Hall, Whitehall, 20, 70.
Jones, James Earl, 237, 285.
Jonson, Ben, 28, 87, 107, 111, 155, 161, 248.
Jordan, Dorothy (Mrs.), 158.

Kahn, Michael, 195, 228, 237, 238, 247, 261.
Kean, Charles, 111, 140, 171, 195, 202.
Kean, Edmund, 158, 162, 163, 179, 181, 182, 183, 196, 200.
Kemble, John Philip, 158, 162, 163, 171, 176, 179, 182, 183, 260.
Kempe, Will, 50, 124.
Kenilworth, 32.
Killigrew, Thomas, 155.
King's Men, 43, 46, 61, 104, 108, 126.
King's Company, 169.
Kline, Kevin, 270.
Kozintsev, Grigori, 227, 247, 267, 269, 271, 276, 277, 278.
Kott, Jan, 227, 241, 242, 258.
Kurosawa, Akira, 269, 271, 272, 275, 276, 277, 278.
Kyd, Thomas, 57, 111; *Spanish Tragedy*, 48.
Kyle, Barry, 263.
Kynaston, Edward, 164.

Laforgue, Jules, 189.
Laneham, John, 34.
Langham, Michael, 238.
Langtree, Lily, 144.
Lapotaire, Jane, 286.
Laughton, Charles, 190, 214.
Leavis, F. R., 250.
Leicester Guildhall, 61.
Lepage, Robert, 236, 238.
locations, see sets, under: theatres, Elizabethan.
London Shakespeare performances (post 1890), 199, 204, 212.
Lord Admiral's Men, 43, 87.
Lord Chamberlain's Men, 43, 46, 61, 108, 114.
Lord Leicester's Company, 61.
Lords of Misrule, 113.
Lords' Room, 29.
Lowin, John, 174.
Lyceum Theatre, 146, 222.

Macklin, Charles, 130.
Macready, William Charles, 144, 158, 171, 177, 179, 182, 196, 200.
Maddermarket Theatre, Norwich, 249.
make-up, 38.
managers, 31, 49, 152 (see individual names).
Mankind, 33, 124.
Mansfield, Richard, 144.
Mantell, Robert, 144.
manuscript plays, 36a, 45, 106.
Marlowe, Christopher, 33, 34, 69, 101, 150, 209, 248; *Dr. Faustus*, 48.
Marlowe, Julia, 144.
Marowitz, Charles, 189, 244, 257.
Marry, Anne Brunton, 144.
Marston, John, 107.
Marxism, 110, 123, 233, 242, 250, 254.
Maryland, 172, 196.
Mason, Brewster, 265.
Massinger, Philip, 107, 155.

Master of the Revels, 39, 41.
McCullough, Christopher, 250.
McCullough, John, 144.
McKellen, Ian, 251, 266a, 279, 286.
medieval drama, 33, 34, 72, 123, 124.
Mendelssohn, Felix, 129.
Mendes, Sam, 251.
Mermaid Theatre, 53.
Messina, Cedric, 275, 280, 285.
Method acting, 28, 129, 200.
Middle Temple, 106.
Middleton, Thomas, 107.
Miller, Jonathan, 153, 228, 247, 250, 259, 263, 274, 275, 285.
Mississippi and Mississippi Valley, 131, 172, 196.
Mobile, Alabama, 172, 196.
Modjeska, Helena, 144.
Molyneux, Paul, 192.
Monk, Nugent, 249.
morality plays, 33, 123.
Moscow (Craig's *Hamlet*), 201.
Moshinsky, Elijah, 285.
Mucedorus, 48.
multi-culturalism, 244.
Munday, Anthony, 107.
music, 12, 20, 21, 22, 47, 60, 85, 91, 93, 94, 97, 129, 139, 141, 149, 167, 172, 180, 202, 211, 284.
My Own Private Idaho, 266a.
mystery plays, 113, 123, 292.

Nashe, Thomas, 107.
National Theatre, U.K., 209, 248, 251, 264, 279.
Neoclassicism, 160, 174, 178.
New Critics, 28, 250, 289.
New Historicism, 39, 110.
New Orleans, 196.
New York, 207.
New York African Shakespeare Company, 192.
New York Shakespeare Festival, 253.
New York Times, 253.

Newcastle, Duchess of, 155,
Newington Butts Theatre, 43, 51.
Nietzsche, Friedrich, 28.
Noble, Adrian, 238, 240, 247, 263.
Norden, John, 70.
North Carolina, 172, 196.
Northern Broadsides Company, 251.
Nunn, Trevor, 186, 228, 239, 241, 244, 248, 250, 263, 264, 270, 286.
Nursery Theatre, 169.

oaths, 261.
Odessa (Texas), 196.
Ohio Valley, 131, 172.
Old Vic Theatre, 126, 187, 190, 198, 212, 214, 215, 216, 230, 236, 246.
Oldcastle, Sir John, 39.
Olivier, Laurence, 129, 133, 219, 230, 248, 265, 269, 270, 271, 272, 276, 278, 280, 284, 292.
opera, 97, 125, 141, 169, 181, 232, 279.
Oregon Shakespeare Festival, 207, 230.
Orgel, Stephen, 111, 264.
Orlando (Florida), 196.
Orlando Furioso, 45.
Oxford, 36a.

pageantry, 32, 34, 122.
Papp, Joseph, 6, 189, 192, 239, 253, 261.
Paris, 252.
Pasco, Richard, 138, 231, 265.
patronage, 36, 36a, 104.
Paul's Theatre, 43.
Payne, Ben Iden, 207, 230.
Pembroke's Men, 46.
Pennington, Michael, 231, 286.
Pepys, Samuel, 164.
personnel, 36a.
Petrarch, 122.

Phelps, Samuel, 171, 200, 223.
Phillips, Robin, 228.
Phoenix Theatre, 43, 169.
Pickford, Mary, 260.
pillars, 74, 118, 293.
plague, 61.
Plantagenets, The, 238.
players, see actors.
Plato, 28.
Playfair, Giles, 221.
Plautus, 292.
playwrights (see also individual names), 28, 30, 36a, 55, 69, 72, 107, 155, 197.
plot summaries, 35, 45.
Plummer, Christopher, 237.
Poel, William, 137, 191, 195, 204, 207, 209, 210, 211, 221, 222, 232, 234, 246, 249.
Polanski, Roman, 240, 276.
Pollard, Thomas, 174.
Pope, Elizabeth, 158.
Porter's Hall Theatre, 43.
Potter, John, 166.
Pre-Raphaelites, 202.
private theatres (see also individual names), 27, 29, 34, 43, 52, 60, 70, 84, 97, 102, 116, 154, 156.
prompt books, 35, 45, 106, 134, 145.
prompter, 118.
properties, see entry under theatres, Elizabethan.
Prospero's Books, 266a.
psychology, psychiatry, 42, 116, 242, 250, 254, 269, 272.
publication, 4, 30, 31, 35, 36a, 172.
puritans, 28, 42, 44, 50, 92.

Quayle, Antony, 186, 280, 282.
Queen's Men, 43.
Quinn, James, 163.

race, 266a, 277 (see Africa, *Merchant of Venice*).

Reardon, Michael, 251.
Red Bull Theatre, 43, 68, 169.
Red Lion Theatre, 43.
Redgrave, Vanessa, 244.
Rees, Roger, 231.
Regent's Park Open Air Theatre, 212, 214.
Reinhardt, Max, 129, 146, 195, 269, 276.
repertory, 33, 36a, 108, 243.
Revels Office, see Master of the Revels.
Rhenanus, Johannes, 107.
rhetoric, 36a, 53, 101.
Richardson, Ian, 138, 265.
Richardson, Ralph, 218, 245, 248.
rival companies, 169.
Robeson, Paul, 192.
Robson, Flora, 214.
Roman classical theatre, 292.
Rose Theatre, 20, 43, 74, 76, 78, 86.
Rousseau, Jean Jacques, 28.
Royal Shakespeare Company (see also Stratford), 148, 186, 187, 227, 236, 242, 246, 250, 262, 263, 279.
Rylance, Mark, 64, 293.

Sacramento, 205.
Sadler's Wells Theatre, 200.
Saint Evremond, Charles de, 180.
Salisbury Court Theatre, 43, 65, 169.
San Francisco, 205.
Satyr Upon Players, A, 164.
Scales, Prunella, 282.
scene structure & sequences, see act divisions.
Schell, Maximilian, 270.
Scofield, Paul, 248.
scripts, 3, 21, 24, 35, 38, 95, 101, 117, 121, 135, 149, 155, 203, 220, 238, 266, 266a, 275, 281.
Sellars, Peter, 153.
Serlio, Sebastiano, 66, 70.

Shadwell, Thomas, 168.
Shakespeare Wallah, 22, 66a.
Shakespeare, William, as director, 99, 107, 118, 204.
Shakespeare, William (works)
—*As You Like It*, 54, 96, 111a, 149, 220, 223, 231, 238, 244, 254, 263, 285.
—*All's Well*, 96, 213, 228, 231, 238, 263.
—*Antony*, 103, 104, 124, 138, 191, 192, 200, 202, 238, 239, 241, 252, 260, 274, 285, 286.
—*Comedy of Errors*, 54, 88, 285.
—*Coriolanus*, 104, 127, 139, 175, 181, 182, 191, 203, 227, 241, 265, 286.
—*Cymbeline*, 11, 89, 152, 191, 194, 202, 203, 220, 231, 238, 263, 264.
—*Hamlet*, 21, 37, 53, 57, 58, 85, 88, 89, 92, 99, 102, 104, 113, 115, 116, 124, 127, 129, 132, 138, 146, 147, 150, 152, 158, 176, 180, 181, 188, 189, 191, 194, 200, 201, 203, 206, 207, 209, 219, 220, 227, 230, 231, 233, 235, 238, 239, 245, 248, 258, 259, 265, 266a, 269, 270, 271, 272, 273, 276, 277, 279, 284, 286, 291.
—*1 Henry IV*, 33, 37, 39, 63, 102, 124, 132, 152, 161, 173, 220, 241, 276, 277, 280, 292.
—*2 Henry IV*, 33, 39, 63, 124, 280, 287, 292.
—*Henry V*, 52, 99, 103, 114, 122, 124, 132, 149, 177, 191, 219, 227, 237, 260, 266a, 269, 271, 273, 275, 276, 280, 284, 285, 286, 292.
—*Henry VI*, 92, 103, 122, 187, 228, 229, 275 (see *The Plantagenets*, *The Wars of the Roses*).
—*Henry VIII*, 24, 57, 88, 91, 114, 139, 140, 147, 152, 167, 185, 202, 209, 214, 233, 260, 285.
—*John*, 152, 182, 233, 241, 279, 286.
—*Julius Caesar*, 88, 114, 115, 127, 152, 173, 182, 191, 200, 202, 238, 241, 258, 273, 278, 286.
—*Lear*, 37, 89, 92, 96, 99, 102, 103, 104, 109, 111, 119, 129, 132, 139, 152, 157, 161, 164, 166, 173, 181, 182, 188, 189, 191, 200, 203, 206, 209, 216, 227, 233, 238, 239, 245, 252, 254, 259, 266a, 267, 271, 272, 273, 274, 275, 276, 277.
—*Love's Labour's Lost*, 89, 91, 99, 114, 122, 124, 152, 191, 285, 286.
—*Macbeth*, 22, 53, 57, 85, 91, 95, 103, 104, 113, 115, 122, 146, 147, 149, 151, 152, 162, 164, 167, 173, 176, 177, 181, 185, 188, 189, 191, 192, 200, 203, 206, 207, 209, 213, 224, 233, 238, 240, 248, 258, 260, 263, 269, 271, 272, 273, 276.
—*Measure for Measure*, 104, 109, 122, 139, 207, 210, 211, 220, 223, 238, 244, 252, 258, 260, 263.
—*Merchant of Venice*, 88, 89, 94, 100, 130, 146, 149, 152, 153, 158, 173, 179, 191, 192, 203, 206, 209, 231, 233, 238, 257, 259, 274, 286, 287.
—*Merry Wives*, 54, 152, 164, 224

—*Midsummer Night's Dream*, 57, 91, 92, 100, 109, 114, 122, 124, 129, 152, 191, 228, 234, 236, 238, 239, 241, 252, 254, 259, 269, 270, 273, 276, 278.
—*Much Ado*, 37, 91, 100, 124, 170, 182, 187, 203, 206, 207, 214, 216, 233, 239, 241, 244, 245, 281, 293.
—*Othello*, 33, 92, 103, 129, 133, 146, 147, 152, 167, 170, 173, 177, 179, 181, 182, 188, 191, 192, 194, 196, 200, 203, 216, 219, 233, 237, 241, 257, 259, 266a, 267, 269, 270, 271, 272, 273, 276, 285.
—*Pericles*, 22, 52, 57, 91, 200, 224, 264.
—*Richard II*, 32, 37, 89, 122, 127, 138, 177, 181, 202, 235, 238, 241, 265, 274, 280, 287.
—*Richard III*, 24, 33, 61, 88, 92, 103, 114, 115, 116, 122, 146, 152, 162, 166, 167, 173, 177, 179, 182, 200, 203, 219, 220, 228, 238, 251, 266a, 271, 273, 275, 276, 279, 284, 286, 291.
—*Romeo*, 38, 52, 53, 91, 119, 124, 132, 138, 140, 146, 168, 181, 182, 187, 191, 203, 206, 209, 228, 231, 234, 272, 276.
—*Taming of the Shrew*, 152, 194, 207, 216, 238, 239, 244, 250, 257, 258, 259, 260, 261, 263, 266a, 273, 274, 276, 285.
—*Tempest*, 54, 57, 104, 109, 122, 127, 164, 173, 189, 195, 207, 228, 231, 236, 245, 251, 252, 254, 256, 259, 264, 269.
—*Timon*, 22, 91, 139, 164, 168, 182, 200, 231, 252, 260.
—*Titus*, 11, 48, 192, 238, 241, 260, 285.
—*Troilus*, 35, 88, 124, 138, 168, 209, 211, 227, 251, 259, 260, 285, 286.
—*Twelfth Night*, 37, 54, 85, 88, 96, 102, 104, 106, 109, 111a, 139, 152, 182, 191, 203, 213, 220, 227, 230, 231, 235, 238, 244, 265, 286, 287.
—*Two Gentlemen*, 4, 114, 124.
—*Two Noble Kinsmen*, 97, 256.
—*Winter's Tale*, 139, 191, 200, 202, 231, 238, 264, 286.
Shaw, Fiona, 263.
Shaw, G. B., 189, 210.
Sher, Antony, 153, 228.
Shirley, James, 155.
showboats, 172.
Siddons, Sarah, 147, 158, 162, 163, 167, 176, 182, 185, 188, 209.
silences, 95, 102, 109, 117, 150.
Sinden, Donald, 231, 241, 265.
sitting on stage, 29.
Skelton, John, 33.
Sly, William, 50.
Smith, Morgan, 192.
soliloquies, 38, 90, 118, 119, 121, 150, 286.
songs, 12, 20, 97, 122, 160 (see music).
Sothern, Edward, 144.
Spottiswoode, Patrick, 293.
Stafford-Clark, Max, 238.
stage directions, 21, 24, 35, 72, 89, 94, 97, 106, 118, 127, 145, 150.
Stanislavsky, Constantin, 28, 146, 258.
Stevenson, Juliet, 263.
Stewart, Patrick, 231, 286.
Stoppard, Tom, 249.
Strange's (Lord Derby's) Men, 46.
Stratford (Connecticut), 237.
Stratford (Ontario), 215, 264.

Stratford-upon-Avon theatres (Memorial Theatre, Swan, Other Place; see also Royal Shakespeare Co.), 187, 194, 197, 204, 207, 215, 216, 222, 225, 235, 244, 251, 252, 262, 265.
Strehle, Giorgio, 195, 228, 256.
Suchet, David, 231, 286.
Sullivan, Sir Arthur, 202.
Suzman, Janet, 270.
Swan Theatre (London), 43.
Swinarski, Konrad, 228.
Syndicate (theatrical), 144.

Tarlton, Richard, 19, 34, 43, 50, 124.
Tate, Nahum, 166, 170, 173, 182, 187, 188.
Tatham, John, 155.
Taylor, Joseph, 174.
Tearle, Godfrey, 233.
Teatro Lyrico, Milan, 195.
television, see films and video.
Tennis Court Theatre, 170.
Terry, Ellen, 190, 201, 202, 211, 222.
Texas, 172, 196, 207.
Theatre, The (Shoreditch), 43, 51, 72, 74, 82, 120.
Theatre Royal, 212.
theatres, Elizabethan (overviews), 2, 5, 12, 13, 16, 17, 20, 25, 26, 36a, 43, 48, 55, 60, 67, 72, 82, 85, 87, 93, 125, 126, 140 (see also named theatres).
　　—conventions, 2, 15, 18, 25, 26, 38, 48, 60, 147, 281.
　　—economics 49, 51, 85, 87, 108, 155, 170.
　　—lighting, 27, 38, 60, 70, 93, 98, 111, 119, 139, 149, 179.
　　—machinery, 66, 74.
　　—properties, 27, 36a, 38, 49, 60, 72, 85, 89, 90, 93, 94, 98, 106, 117, 118, 121, 135, 150, 157, 291.
　　—repertory, 33, 108.
　　—sets/settings 27, 38, 60, 66, 70, 72, 90, 93, 94, 106, 139, 149, 211.
　　—sound effects, 25, 93, 115, 149, 220, 291.
　　—stage business, 25, 37, 38, 78, 94, 117, 135, 147, 150, 220, 236, 247.
　　—structure, 2, 48, 60, 65, 71, 72, 74, 78, 81, 85, 118, 154.
theatres, Jacobean, 14, 125, 126, 140, 154, 155, 156, 157, 174.
theatres, post-Restoration, 125, 126, 130, 131, 140, 165, 166, 167, 170, 173, 174, 177, 178, 180.
theatres, 18th-century, 125, 126, 130, 131, 140, 160, 161, 165, 166, 167, 168.
Thorndike, Sybil, 190, 214.
Tokyo Globe Theatre, 251.
touring, 31, 61, 122, 140, 144, 202, 216, 222, 230.
transvestism, 28, 31, 34, 35, 42, 43, 44, 92, 111a, 114, 121, 141, 151, 163, 174, 236, 272.
Tree, Beerbohm, 129, 137, 146, 190, 202, 204, 208, 210, 217, 269, 279.
Tucker, Patrick, 95.
Tudor drama, 33, 72, 156.
tyring house, 43, 81.

United Company, 169.
unities, the, 66, 160, 166, 178.
universities, 34, 36a, 66, 69, 70, 81.

Vaughan, Stuart, 261.
Venice, 54.
Verdi, Giuseppe, 141.
Vermeer, Jan, 274, 285.
Veronese, Paolo, 274, 285.

Index

verse, 54, 95, 134, 286, 287.
Vice figures, 33.
Victoria and Albert Museum, 206.
video (and television), 2, 99, 143, 146, 153, 218, 238, 239, 242, 250, 259, 268, 269, 270, 274, 275, 279, 280, 281, 282, 283, 285, 286, 288, 290, 292, 293.
Virginia, 172, 196.
Vitagraph Shakespeare, 279.
Vitruvius, 64, 66.

Walter, Harriet, 262.
Wanamaker, Sam, 77, 78, 121, 250, 292.
Warner, David, 265.
Warner, Deborah, 238.
Wars of the Roses (R.S.C.), 187, 225, 235, 242, 246; Bogdanov, 229, 242.
Watteau, Jean-Antoine, 285.
Webb, John, 66.

Webster, John, 57; *Duchess of Malfi*, 260.
Webster, Margaret, 146.
Welles, Orson, 146, 189, 190, 192, 240, 247, 255, 264, 267, 269, 271, 272, 276, 278; *Chimes at Midnight*, 245, 271, 278, 280.
White, Liz, 272.
Whitefriars Theatre, 43.
Wilders, John, 249, 283.
Williams, Clifford, 225.
Williams, Harcourt, 198, 249.
Willis, Elizabeth, 167.
Woffington, Pegg, 163.
Wolfit, Sir Donald, 190, 216.
Wood, Charles, 192.

Zadek, Peter, 195.
zanni, 54.
Zeffirelli, Franco, 137, 235, 266a, 270, 272, 276, 278.